Praise for Josep

Joseph Clough is one of those wise people who seems to know exactly what makes people tick and how to help people to be the most they can be. I'm sure by reading this book you'll take giant steps towards being your potential.

– **David Hamilton, bestselling author of *How Your Mind Can Heal Your Body* and *The Contagious Power of Thinking***

Joseph gets to the heart of you and your potential. If you ever wonder to yourself about how you can be, do and have more in your life, this book provides you with a soul-centred and effective solution. You can live your potential starting today, and Joseph will be your excellent guide.

– **Alexandra Watson, leading Happiness Coach, success mentor and bestselling author**

Joseph provides a rare and articulate insight, his words and philosophy resonate deeply in these times of change, he is a true master of communication and brings great inspiration to many with his words of wisdom.

– **Tim Wheater, award-winning composer**

Joseph Clough is an inspiration. In this book he gives us the tools we need to become all that we can be. He encourages us to dare to dream and then to live the dream.

– **Tim Freke, author of *The Mystery Experience* and *How Long is Now?***

Joseph Clough's *Be Your Potential* helps you to do exactly that. It offers powerful insights and exercises for bridging the gap between where you are now and being your potential to make things even better. Joseph Clough is a master at what he does, but what makes him be his potential so effectively is that he genuinely cares about making a positive difference to the lives of others.

– **Sandy C. Newbigging, author of *Mind Calm*** and meditation teacher

BE YOUR POTENTIAL

BE YOUR POTENTIAL

You **already** have everything you need.
You just need to **know** how to use it!

JOSEPH CLOUGH

HAY HOUSE

Carlsbad, California • New York City • London • Sydney
Johannesburg • Vancouver • Hong Kong • New Delhi

First published and distributed in the United Kingdom by:
Hay House UK Ltd, Astley House, 33 Notting Hill Gate, London W11 3JQ
Tel: +44 (0)20 3675 2450; Fax: +44 (0)20 3675 2451 www.hayhouse.co.uk

Published and distributed in the United States of America by:
Hay House, Inc., PO Box 5100, Carlsbad, CA 92018-5100.
Tel.: (1) 760 431 7695 or (800) 654 5126; F
ax: (1) 760 431 6948 or (800) 650 5115. www.hayhouse.com

Published and distributed in Australia by:
Hay House Australia Ltd, 18/36 Ralph St, Alexandria NSW 2015.
Tel.: (61) 2 9669 4299; Fax: (61) 2 9669 4144. www.hayhouse.com.au

Published and distributed in the Republic of South Africa by:
Hay House SA (Pty), Ltd, PO Box 990, Witkoppen 2068.
Tel./Fax: (27) 11 467 8904. www.hayhouse.co.za

Published and distributed in India by:
Hay House Publishers India, Muskaan Complex, Plot No.3, B-2,
Vasant Kunj, New Delhi – 110 070. Tel.: (91) 11 4176 1620;
Fax: (91) 11 4176 1630. www.hayhouse.co.in

Distributed in Canada by:
Raincoast, 9050 Shaughnessy St, Vancouver, BC V6P 6E5.
Tel.: (1) 604 323 7100; Fax: (1) 604 323 2600

© Joseph Clough 2012
This edition published 2014

The moral rights of the author have been asserted.

The information given in this book should not be treated as a substitute
for professional medical advice; always consult a medical practitioner.
Any use of information in this book is at the reader's discretion and
risk. Neither the author nor the publisher can beheld responsible for
any loss, claim or damage arising out of the use, or misuse, or the
suggestions made or the failure to take medical advice.

A catalogue record for this book is available from the British Library.

ISBN 978-1-78180-250-2

Printed and bound in Great Britain by TJ International Ltd.

MIX
Paper from
responsible sources
FSC
www.fsc.org   FSC® C013056

Dedicated to my late Grandmother, Olive Clough, who will always be my shining light and my inspiration.

Also dedicated with love and thanks to:

My parents, Paul and Susan, who have given me all the support and unconditional love that any son could ever wish for.

To my brothers Luke and Daniel, who have always been there for me.

My Grandfather Gerald, the kindest man I know.

My closest friends, you all know who you are.

Finally, to the Creation of Your Future.

CONTENTS

RE-REMEMBERING THE FUTURE

I want to tell you something;
it may just be something.

I want to tell you about a special person, my friend, who only knew what had been taught to them. This person was someone who struggled at times – struggled with themselves and how they lived in this world – like most people living today.

For this person, there was so much external pressure from society that they lost who they really were – like most people living today.

But who was this person?

As a child, they thought everything was possible. It wasn't hard. As a child they thought they could be, do or have whatever they wanted, and it was as if there were no limitations inside them – just boundless thinking.

They lived in the moment and just knew everything would be how they wanted it to be – with a career they loved that would fulfill their ambitions, an ideal family and home – and that they would enjoy the sort of wonderful life of which we all dream.

But as time went on, something happened. Those beautiful dreams were eroded. It was as if the older my friend grew, the more they forgot about how their life would be perfect. Experience taught them that they had to live a certain way. Look a certain way. Act in a certain way.

People said they had to be realistic. They had to 'get real'.

They couldn't be the person they thought they would be, as they were told they were 'living in a fantasy world'. They began to buy into the external pressures, like everyone else. They began to buy into the opinions of everyone around them and society's expectations of how they *should* be.

These people – and even society – thought they were right, but they didn't know any better as *they too* were once that child who dreamed boundless dreams but were told they had to 'get real'.

A few years later, my friend began to look back at their memories, and their experiences told them how they should act in the future – the past was the only definite thing they knew after all.

My friend began to make decisions based on what they thought was real and true. Over time, those memories, thoughts and decisions created beliefs – beliefs they thought were true, as past experience told them so.

Unfortunately, this led to the creation of the belief, 'I'm not good enough', and at times they feared rejection and failure. It was as if the more they lived, the more they created limiting beliefs of how they viewed the world, and more importantly, how they viewed themselves.

They began to settle for second best. A job they didn't like, being with the wrong people and not able to find the right partner.

At times they thought they should settle for what they had been given in their life – 'accept the cards' they had been dealt and their 'lot' in life. These beliefs and values were not what they wanted, but their inner thoughts simply fed their ever-growing and ingrained beliefs of not being allowed what they wanted.

I wonder what would have happened to my friend if they had kept hold of, or could regain, their childlike inner curiosity and the belief that they could do, be, or have what they wanted.

My friend didn't know that they were simply asleep – asleep to the truth.

They simply bought into their own – and others' – expectations of just getting by and struggling.

What if that person knew that whatever they thought they were, they were actually even more beautiful, inside and out? In fact, no matter what they thought they were, they always were and will be more than that.

What if they realized that past experiences were just an illusion of the mind's creation? And that the beliefs they held about the world were self-made illusions. And that the fear and worry they had was an illusion.

An illusion?

Yes, an illusion. It's not real. It's a matter of perception.

Their perception was not reality. When people said 'get real', that person was actually getting less 'real' and more fake.

When you go deeper, a person – broken down to their smallest parts – is just energy. Energy that vibrates.

Energy that moves and has taken form as a living, breathing person.

And if they are simply energy, at the smallest level of existence, that would mean everything around them is the same – just energy. The people in their life are energy; the physical things around them are condensed energy.

If that were true, it would mean that everything is a sea of energy, going into and out of form, through birth to death; in and out of form, forever energy – transforming from one form to the other, but always energy. To realize that they were truly interconnected with all that is, and ever will be.

What?

You see this person didn't realize that they were everything that was around them. They saw themselves as separate, as an individual cut off from the world, separated from people and things. But it wasn't their fault they were thinking that way – it was what they had been taught, after all.

But there was still more to re-remember that would shock and anger them, and cause them to even refuse to believe.

All the things they didn't like in others were simply a reflection of what they had within themselves.

The wonderful qualities they saw in others were also wonderful qualities in themselves. In fact, this person was like a small part within the whole of everything else. But what they didn't realize was that everything else, the whole, was in them.

The fear only existed in this person through them not being the *real* them. Fear was when they were not being the real them – their true potential. They didn't realize that life begins on the edge of our comfort zone. Fear was the thing that separated them from everything else they wanted to be.

But fear was all my friend knew. It wasn't their fault; it was what they had been taught.

It makes you wonder whether fear is a manmade creation, doesn't it?

And whether time itself is manmade.

We give life to time, to fear, to beliefs and, even, to ourselves and the world around us.

Fear feeds fear and it spreads like wildfire. Fear causes us to focus on what we don't want to happen, which causes us to focus on and give life to more fear.

But if fear is a creation of ourselves, what are we really?

We are love.

Love is the only thing we really are – the only thing that exists. Everything else is an illusion.

Love transcends everything; even things we feel we cannot change. Love is something which, if you lived and breathed it in every moment, would give you optimism and the knowledge that all is well and all is right and always will be.

When love is fully present in you, everything pans out how it should – like the dreams and hopes of a child. Having pure joy and love allows you to actualize what you want. Some people may say that love is a simple chemical reaction in our brain. This is also true, but it does not mean it's any less real.

To re-remember the time before time – a time when everything just *was*. When there was no separation, just a place where everything *was* everything. But in order to make sense of what we were, we had to realize what we were not.

To give meaning to ourselves and the things we saw, we began to judge and label our experience, to make sense of the world we live in. Like light and dark, light can only exist with darkness.

But this person tried to make too much sense of what they saw around them, and who they were themselves. This person didn't realize that separating themselves from what was not them was a lie – yes, a lie.

Because they were *everything*.

This person didn't realize that they were love and the fear they held was an illusion. Or that everything they saw in the world was an illusion, other than love.

If that person realized how beautiful and wonderful they really were, they could create what they wished for most in the world – to be themselves. They would look through the eyes of love, and accept nothing less than bliss.

Then they could live the life they wanted, just as they had thought as a child – a life free of boundaries and limitations.

If my friend had a choice – was able to choose – they would no longer have to buy into others' expectations to be a certain way. They would no longer be asleep. They would re-awaken and re-remember what they were meant to remember.

Rather than being a product of life, they could allow life to be a product of what they created. They were love in its purest form.

You see, this person is the most wonderful person. This person is pure love, and is beautiful exactly the way they really are.

That is what is real – the real them.

For this friend to finally realize that they are the ultimate, that they are the part and the whole, that the world they see around them is a mere reflection of themselves.

That they could choose to create the life they want; that they no longer have to settle for second best.

They could be who they want to be.

That they know at the smallest part of themselves, that they are love, and to the largest thing, that they are love.

The type of love I'm talking about changes everything. Not just the label of love, which we have become accustomed to, but a deeper love. Love not just for someone else, but also for all, and especially for ourselves.

They are the light that can light up the illusory darkness.

When they realized this – felt it, breathed it – and just knew that they are the greatest gift, that they are the most beautiful of things in the world, they realized that person is...

You.

WHAT IT MEANS TO LIVE TO YOUR TRUE POTENTIAL

Living to your true potential means being free of limitations and opening your mind to the infinite possibilities that exist within you. It all starts with the decision that now is the time to unleash the power of you. No matter what psychological or emotional issues you may have. Right now, think of your desires and aspirations and imagine how your life would change dramatically if you knew exactly how to make them a reality. I know that when you apply the following wisdom to your life your limitations will cease to exist. Now is the time to awaken your mind, body and soul to all the success you deserve.

And you do deserve it. In fact, I know in every way you are 100 per cent worthy and good enough to succeed in anything you wish to do, without fear or doubt. It all starts now – this moment – and your decision to go on this journey with me to understand the deeper nature of you, so that you can create changes in yourself and your life whenever you desire. In other words, to learn the secrets of being your potential.

To make the journey effortless for you, I have designed and created a series of mind-changing audio tracks so I can coach you to be your potential you. They are:

- *The Perfect Health*
- *Amazing Relationships*
- *Financial Abundance*
- *General Manifestation*
- *Positive Affirmations*
- *Power of Focus*
- *Change Your Emotional State Process*
- *Negative Emotion Release Process*
- *Becoming the You, You Wish To Be*

You can play or download these audio tracks for free at www.josephclough.com/byp as you read through the book. These are life-changing coaching and hypnotic audio processes that will cause you to make profound changes consciously and unconsciously. It's important that you only listen to them when they are mentioned in the book, as they will guide you each step of the way, exactly when you need them.

Life is meant to be magnificent, rewarding and joyful and I want to show you how you can have it all.

Working as an international trainer and therapist, my goal in life is to help people achieve their full potential and ultimately reach peace, happiness and confidence in life. I am also a trainer in hypnotherapy, coaching and neuro-linguistic programming (NLP), and my work has taken me to some amazing places in the world.

For the last ten years I have strived to get my message out to as many people as possible, because I feel it's our duty to share knowledge and to contribute to the world and help those in need. I have done this through my popular free podcast, free mobile apps and online programmes, and have given away over 70 hours of free audio and video on how to be your potential. These have reached more than 500,000 people around the globe in under two years. My mission is simple: to help as many people as possible.

But let's be clear. At one time my life wasn't joyful or magnificent. In fact, it was quite the opposite. I remember a time when I felt completely lost in life. Everything I wanted felt out of my reach and beyond my control. It felt like life was dictating my unhappiness. I wasn't living the life I wanted or dreamed of as a child.

Have you ever been there?

I think we've all been there at one point or another, wanting something deeper. For some it may be finding inner peace or contentment, for others it's the material things that life has to offer – good health, the ideal career or our true soulmate. Or perhaps we want to feel worthy, to know we are good enough and to love ourselves unconditionally.

When I got to that point of feeling so lost and unhappy, I knew something had to change in my life. When I made that conscious decision to change my life, something began to happen inside me. I made a commitment to myself to become the 'real me', and on that journey towards 'me' I discovered the truth about who I am and also the truth about how we can fulfil our true potential. That truth truly changed my world. From confusion came clarity, from despair came self-worth and from lack came abundance – in all areas of my life.

It may seem hard to believe, but it happened, and I can show you the deeper truth of you. I can teach you how to be the real you, full of happiness, love and fulfillment. That might sound like a bold promise, but I want nothing less than that for you. But first, I have some questions for you:

What do you want out of life?

How do you want your health to be?

Do you want financial abundance?

What type of relationships do you want?

Do you want success and love in all areas of your life?

In the following pages you will discover the truth and knowledge you need to achieve your true desires and outcomes. I believe that life is meant to be good, but that our true intentions get lost along the way, as we are programmed by our past experiences, educators, friends, and even our parents and partners. For many of us, as we go through life we develop limiting beliefs about ourselves and even the world, and unhealthy mindsets. But keeping hold of negative emotions and poor behaviours can mean that we are not able to generate the success we desire in our life.

To put it simply – we've been programmed by our life experiences. We have bought into other people's expectations and they have become our own. But don't worry, it can and will be undone. Now is your time to reclaim your potential and truly be the person you wish to be – the real you.

Some of the things I will say may push your buttons and highlight new thoughts that will make you re-evaluate your perceptions about life. But you can choose: stop now and carry on the way you always have done or let this be the time when your whole world changes. So, whatever the reason you bought this book, something has to change and now is the time to do it.

I believe in synchronicity. When you really want to change, the opportunity will arise, and I believe this is the opportunity to achieve all the things you've ever wanted. And I can tell you now that I am going to give you 100 per cent of me. I am going to teach you everything I know about getting the happiness and results that you deserve. If you can match that, and really put in 100 per cent of yourself, I just know – in fact, I guarantee – that you will get *all* the results that you've ever wanted, and more.

No matter what age you are, no matter what you think you can't achieve, I know that you can achieve it. Some people may tell you to 'be realistic', but I ask you: who defines what is realistic? That's right, we are the only ones who can make that judgement, no one else can do that for us – unless we accept others' expectations of being 'realistic' to be true. I think it's safe to say that the biggest breakthroughs and achievements the world has seen to date were once deemed unrealistic, but the people who achieved them went by their personal realistic expectations, not those of others. In fact, I *know* that you can achieve more than you think you can, because I firmly believe everyone can.

One more question: are you ready to be your potential?

CHAPTER ONE

SOMETHING HAS TO CHANGE AND NOW IS THE TIME TO DO IT

I'm pretty sure that you bought this book because you're not quite happy with your life in some way, and you want to be living to your true potential. Maybe you're fed up with having the same unfulfilling relationships, or maybe you don't have the abundance in life that you truly feel you deserve. Perhaps you lack self-worth or confidence, or want to get your health back on track.

The key is, whatever you think you are, you are always more than that and you *are* able to achieve all that you desire, no matter what obstacles you think are in your way. This is the deeper truth that many have forgotten, and now is the time to not only re-remember this universal truth, but to be it and actualize it fully.

In the following chapters I will share some of the wisdom and principles I have learned and developed, which will – if you let them – transform your life and awaken your mind to the deeper truth of you. I use these principles to help people every day, and so far I've helped 500,000 people around the world to achieve their results. And I'm still quite young.

One of the most important principles that I've learned, and one that I teach my clients, is that nothing can stop us but ourselves. I wasn't gifted from a young age – far from it, in fact. I do not say this to impress you, but rather to share with you some of my story of how I was rock bottom in mind and body but re-remembered my potential. In doing so, I turned my life around, harnessed my potential and actualized my dreams in every area of my life, and I want to share the secret of my success with you.

Years ago I saw the world as a place of fear, uncertainty and scarcity. Today I understand that this happens because we aren't taught to live the life we deserve. It begins at a young age and is passed down to us by our parents, our educators and society as a whole. They do their best, but most of us aren't given the information we need to go out into the world and get what we want out of life.

Why? For the simple reason that the people who are our biggest influencers weren't taught this, and so the cycle continues. This is my sole intent in writing this book: to help reconnect 'you' with your source – the source of your potential.

It used to really frustrate me seeing people not having the life that they wanted. It saddened me that many didn't have the health they wanted, whether it was dis-ease, dis-order, depression or anxiety. It hurt me seeing people just going from one bad relationship to the next, being used and abused, or just having unhappy relationships and not finding their soul mates. And it truly disheartened me that people went to work just for the paycheck at the end of the month or, even worse, that the paycheck just allowed them to struggle through life. Not everyone is ready to open his or her mind to a whole new world. But if you are, then in this moment you can choose to unlock what you need within you. We are all perfect, we can still make changes, and that is fine, but within us we have everything we need – we just need to put our attention and intention into it.

I have heard from 'experts' that it can take weeks, months or even years of therapy to change a habit or problem, but I see things differently. It doesn't have to take long. In fact, transformation can take a moment, a realization or an awakening. When you were born you didn't think, 'I'm going to have a poor life; I'm going to lack fulfillment in my life'.

It's just not meant to be that way and my motivation is to be able to help as many people as I truly can.

This is about you as an individual. Life is meant to be good for you. Life is really meant to get you what you want, to have all the learning and the most amazing experiences, to have all that financial abundance, to have perfect health in every way and to have the career of your dreams.

The pages that follow will allow you to get the life you want and unleash your true potential in a matter of *moments or days,* not weeks, months or years.

Of course you're going to have to put effort into it. I'm not going to tell you that it's going to be an easy process. However, I want you to take the wisdom within lightly. I want you to relax and enjoy this process of transformation, the journey to being your potential. The effort you put in will be enjoyable effort, and inspired action will allow you to reap the rewards of all your desires.

It's about changing your perspective on how you think about life, and about how you can create the changes you desire. Your past decisions have led you here; your present decisions will lead you to where you're going. This moment is more powerful than your decisions in the past. It's like when you are driving – you occasionally look in the small rearview mirror (your past), but you're mostly looking out to the big open road in front of you (the future). But you are in the driving seat and wherever you are, you are in the 'now' and driving to your desired destination.

Using the methods outlined in this book, you will notice the powerful transformations beginning to emerge in your thinking, in how you feel and how you behave on a day-to-day basis.

It's about returning to your potential – the potential you were born with. Because who *you* are right now isn't you, your true potential. I remember when I was a young child, I lacked self-confidence; I would blush all the time and become very self-conscious. I wasn't able to be myself, or to have the relationships or life I wanted. I knew if I kept these issues, I wouldn't be able to have the career I wanted either, and I realized that I couldn't live the life I wanted being that 'me'. However, deep down I knew it wasn't the *real* me.

Wanting more out of life

Ever felt that way? That there is more of you waiting to be released? I did, but for some reason I had the behaviours and mindset of an unconfident person. I struggled with school from the start – a common experience for many children – and it was only thanks to the determination of my mother, and after-school tuition, that I was able to get the grades I needed. But, by the time I went to senior school, I was still extremely unconfident. I was fine around my close friends, but when it came to bigger groups, I just lacked the confidence to speak out; the thought of talking in front of everyone was terrifying.

One time, I remember that a teacher picked on me right in front of everyone, and I felt a blush building up inside of me. I became so self-conscious and could only think, *I've got to get out of here* – but I couldn't. I was stuck in this state of utter embarrassment that seemed to last for eternity. This one event really imprinted a lack of confidence within me and it stayed with me throughout my teenage years. It really held me back as a child.

Having struggled through school, I managed to get the results I needed to get into college – just. But I still didn't know what I wanted to do in my life. Ever been there? I felt unconfident and discontented. I just didn't know where I was going in life. I knew that I wanted more than this. I wanted a life where I felt fulfilled – the one that everyone deserves. So I chose a business course and I thought, *business is going to get me where I want to be, hopefully...*

But guess what? I still felt unhappy, maybe even more so than before. I was stuck. Changing my environment wasn't enough. I had the same negative thoughts, beliefs and feelings. After college, having scraped through my exams, I was fortunate to land a job in insurance. And I say 'fortunate' ironically, because I hated it. It pushed me to the point where I thought, *what am I doing with my life?*

I felt so discontented, and worried about going to work because I didn't want to be there. My finances were in a bad state and my relationships were pretty much non-existent because I was unconfident and insecure. All of that caused my health to suffer as I began eating more and not working out. By the time I was 18 I knew that I didn't want *this* any more and thought, *something has to change and now is the time.* So, although it was a very difficult time in my life, it made me think, *I'm going to change it now. I'm going to get what I want out of life.*

It all starts with a decision

When I made that decision, my life began to unfold. I found some life-transforming wisdom that allowed me to find the life I desired, and this is what you'll learn in this book. The processes will allow you – if you let them – to get all the things that you've always wanted in life. I firmly believe that, having bought this book, you have made this decision, too. If not, make it now!

Fortunately, this is going to be an accelerated version, because I 'failed' many times. But the first thing I want you to realize from those so-called failures, is that all failure is simply feedback and learning to get better. What if the following people perceived their failure as truth and stopped going for their dreams? How would the world be different?

Abraham Lincoln

As a young man, Abraham Lincoln went to war as a captain and returned as a private. He was a failure as a businessman and a lawyer, and when he became a politician, his first attempt at legislature was defeated, as was his first attempt to be nominated for Congress, his application to be commissioner of the General Land Office, his senatorial election of 1854, his efforts for the vice-presidency in 1856 and senatorial election in 1858. But that didn't stop him from becoming US president and successfully leading his country through its greatest internal crisis – the American Civil War – preserving the Union and ending slavery.

Winston Churchill

Churchill was defeated in every election for public office until he became Britain's prime minister at the age of 62. He later gave a speech saying, 'Never give in, never give in, never, never, never, never – in nothing, great or small, large or petty – never give in except to convictions of honour and good sense. Never, never, never, never give up.'

Charles Darwin

Darwin gave up a medical career and was told by his father, 'You care for nothing but shooting, dogs and rat catching'. In his autobiography, he wrote, 'I was considered by all my masters, and my father, a very ordinary boy, rather below the common standard of intellect'. Clearly, he evolved.

Thomas Edison
Told by his teachers that he was 'too stupid to learn anything', Edison was fired from his first two jobs for being 'non-productive'. As an inventor, Edison made 10,000 unsuccessful attempts at inventing the light bulb. When a reporter asked, 'How did it feel to fail 10,000 times?' Edison replied, 'I didn't fail 10,000 times. The light bulb was an invention with 10,000 steps'.

Albert Einstein
Einstein didn't speak until he was four and didn't read until he was seven. His parents thought he was 'sub-normal', and one of his teachers described him as 'mentally slow, unsociable, and adrift forever in foolish dreams'. He was expelled from school and was refused admittance to the Zurich Polytechnic School. The rest of his life is – literally – history.

More famous failures!
The world's most famous motor mechanic, Henry Ford, went broke five times before he succeeded. Michael Jordan was dropped from his high school basketball team. Jordan once observed, 'I've failed over and over again in my life. That is why I succeed'. Walt Disney was fired as a

newspaper editor because 'he lacked imagination and had no good ideas'. He went bankrupt several times before he built Disneyland, and the proposed park was rejected by one city on the grounds that it would only attract 'riffraff'. Harrison Ford's studio vice-president dismissed him with, 'You ain't got it kid, you ain't got it… now get out of here'. Michael Caine's headmaster told him, 'You will be a labourer all your life'. Hollywood studio chiefs initially rejected Charlie Chaplin because his pantomime was considered 'nonsense'. Beethoven was described as 'hopeless as a composer' by his teacher. And an incredible 27 publishers rejected Dr Seuss's first book.

There is no such thing as failure until you decide you have failed and you stop going for your dreams.

You're making the decision consciously and unconsciously by continuing to read that now is the time to awaken your mind's potential. Now you can relax and be easy about the rest of the book while opening your mind to get back to returning to your true potential.

Give up your limitations and your 'whys'

But you may be asking yourself questions, right now or even before you picked up this book, such as, 'Why haven't I got my relationships the way I want them?' 'Why me?', 'Why don't I have the finances?', 'Why do I have to struggle?' or 'Why do I have poor health?'

All those thoughts may have come into your mind from time to time in the past. But it's not about that anymore; it's about changing the now and getting what you really want – *now*.

By being present in this moment, your world can change; you have everything you need within you and you can achieve the inner peace and love you crave. In fact, there is nothing to search for externally – it's all within you.

You may have beliefs about yourself, perhaps feeling 'not good enough' or 'not worthy'. Or you may have been taught the self-restricting beliefs that 'money doesn't grow on trees' or 'you've got to struggle to get what you want – no pain, no gain'. These mindsets, beliefs and attitudes were imprinted on you when you were a young child and have continued to be part of your mindset all the way through your adult life, and now those beliefs have set a structure in getting *those* results. Or maybe your beliefs developed after a series of 'failures' or disappointments. Either way, that's all going to change.

I'm offering you the opportunity to give up those limitations and no longer have the 'whys' – the reasons or the excuses about how your life is at the moment. Your past is unimportant; care about the *now* and how to get what you really want out of life *now,* by being the creator of your reality. Let me explain:

Wherever you are right now, *you have created that* in some way.

How your relationships are, *that is your creation.*

How your finances are, *that is your creation.*

How your health is, *that's all your creation.*

Now, before you throw the book through the nearest window, I don't mean it's your fault – because it truly isn't your fault – but in some way, shape or form, you have created your situation. Your present situation has been created by your actions, reactions and decisions in the past.

And I'm not saying that you've created your situation consciously, either. I don't think anyone would choose to have poor relationships, poor health or poor finances. You don't wake up every day and think, 'I'm going to have bad relationships', or 'I'm going to get more in debt', or 'I'm going to be more unhappy in my life' or 'I'm going to find a job I really loathe and hate'.

A lot of these things are *unconscious* decisions imprinted on your unconscious by your experiences in the past. These are the mindsets that were either passed down to you when you were younger, and which have in turn created the beliefs and values you hold, or the behaviours you've picked up through habit, whether they are good or bad. However, whether they are conscious or unconscious creations, you have formed them in some way.

Let me give you one example, as I am sure you are wondering why.

Jane's story

Several years ago I worked with a client who was suffering from depression. She kept on saying: 'It's not my fault I'm like this. It's the abusive relationships I've had. I had a bad relationship with my father. He always used to put me down and said I wasn't good enough so *he* gave me low confidence, *he* made me a nervous wreck, *he* gave me depression, *he* is the reason why I haven't got my life the way I want it.'

I felt differently. In order for her to have those present experiences of neglect and abuse, she had to *accept* her father's beliefs to be true and choose to accept the same situation in her relationships again and again. She had created her behaviours and chose to allow them to become part of her identity.

When her father said she wasn't good enough, at some level she had taken on his perceptions uncritically and thought, 'Yes, that is who I am'. And once again, not consciously but unconsciously, there was a part of her thinking, 'My father saying that to me repeatedly must mean that it is true.' The acceptance of this experience caused her to decide that this is who she was.

Emotional or physical abuse in our formative years can leave us feeling unworthy and depressed – it is only natural – and Jane's experience may resonate with you, to a lesser or greater degree, in some area of your life. I know it did with me. The more I reacted unconfidently, the more I began to believe that 'I wasn't good enough' and 'I was unconfident'.

After each unsuccessful relationship it's easy to think, 'I know what the next one's going to be like; he or she is just going to use and abuse me', or 'men cheat' or 'women cheat'.

These are the kinds of thoughts you may have, because your past relationships have given you expectations for the future and how the next relationship, or business venture – you name it – will be for you. Your past can guide you to where you *don't* want to be and often to the same place again and again. Past residual thoughts, beliefs, behaviours and actions can create your present situation. And that's *great news*, because it means if we change the 'now' we can change the future.

If you've led a life of being in debt, you're going to expect more of the same, aren't you? You're going to expect a bill to come through the letterbox. You're going to expect not to have the money that you deserve, and that expectation prepares you to receive more of the same – more pain and stress. This is one of the things that needs to change: we need to change your expectation, to flip it around so that you expect your true potential. Life is meant to be good to you.

Life is good to you if you choose it to be.

Even if the actual events are completely beyond your control, it is your mindset that determines whether you survive or not.

Viktor Frankl

Viktor was a Holocaust survivor. His wife and parents were deported to the Theresienstadt camp near Prague, while Viktor was sent to four Nazi camps before finally ending up at Auschwitz. On his arrival, the camp's doctor, Josef Mengele, divided the incoming prisoners into two lines. Those in the line moving left were to go to the gas chambers, while those in the line moving right were to be spared. Viktor was directed to join the line moving left, but slipped unnoticed into the other line. Other members of his family were not so fortunate – his wife, parents and other relatives died in concentration camps. Despite everything, Viktor survived and in his book, *Man's Search For Meaning,* he describes how this happened because he was determined and refused to allow his terrible suffering to affect his mindset:

The one thing you can't take away from me is the way I choose to respond to what you do to me. The last of one's freedoms is to choose one's attitude in any given circumstance... When we are no longer able to change a situation – we are challenged to change ourselves.

Your reality is your creation

Understanding that I was in control of my reality – my state of mind – stopped me in my tracks and made me think: *You mean I created these things... the problems in my life? How did I choose to create them?* This concept really pushed against my values, as I'm sure it does with yours. How is it that we create these circumstances? Why would we create things that we dislike, even hate? How do we create these bad situations?

However, when I thought about it deeply – I truly had to be honest with myself (and you do, too) –

and looked back at my past experiences, I found that there were some common themes in my life. These ranged from limiting beliefs, not feeling good enough, or unworthy of having the life that I wanted, to behaviours that reproduced the same outcome time and time again. I couldn't change the past but I knew that I was the only person creating the present.

It goes back to cause and effect. It sounds strange, but think about it: if your life isn't the way that you want it right now – no matter what area of your life it is – it means you're just an effect of your situation.

You become an effect of everything you are going through, by saying, 'Well, it's not my fault, it's this person's fault', or 'It's my boss's fault', or 'It was the way that teacher bullied me', or 'It was my father's fault' or 'my mother's fault'. Or even, 'It's my ill health' or 'this dis-ease or dis-order that has caused me to have bad health'. Unfortunately, those excuses are giving you reasons to maintain your mindset and giving you permission to continue with your negative behaviours. If I'm pushing some of your buttons, that's good. Stay with me.

When we make excuses, we are playing the blame game. We are powerful when we blame people or things for our situation because we believe that they are outside our control. In order to move forward, we must accept that it doesn't matter who was at fault or to blame. By blaming we are reducing our control over the situation, since to move past it we need the person responsible to correct their mistake. But we cannot rely on others to correct whatever's happened in the past. In order to make changes and be powerful, we must assume responsibility. When we do this, we take back control and that gives us the power to change our situation. Remember, the past is the past: it's over and no longer exists in the present. Refuse to give your power and energy away to the past. Instead, realize that when you take responsibility for your life right now, you take back control and become truly aligned to achieve your goals and desires and therefore change your future.

By having reasons or excuses, you are reaffirming where you already are in life. And the more you reaffirm those reasons or excuses, the more of the 'bad stuff' you're going to get.

So, if you're on the 'effect' side of life, you're pushing the responsibility outside of yourself and onto external things or people, and allowing every situation to be an external fault rather than your own. It gives you those excuses, and those excuses become your reasons as to why you haven't got your life the way you'd like it. And the more you reaffirm those reasons, the more they just put you steadily where you already are – getting the results you've already got.

However, it doesn't have to be that way. You may not be able to change the past, but you can change the way you see it, and more importantly, you can change the now. Are you ready to start changing the now?

All your past experiences have led you up to this pinnacle of your life where everything has to change and will change. All of those past residual behaviours are continuing to produce the effects and the results right now, and will continue to produce them in the future if you carry on the same way.

However, if you change the now and change your mind – and therefore your outcome – that becomes your past and will create the most wonderful *now* in this present moment. So, by making this choice today – by taking responsibility for all you are and everything in your life in the most joyous and empowering way – positive outcomes will unfold for you. You will find opportunities that will start to make changes in the very fibre of your neurology, in the most wonderful way that you could ever imagine.

Take the opportunity right now to take responsibility for your cause and effect.

If you get on the 'cause' side of the equation, you become the cause of all your actions. You become the cause of everything that you've done and all that you're about to do. The decision will empower you by giving you responsibility and opportunity. You begin to own the situation, and you begin to own your life. How amazing would it be to know that you're in control? Wouldn't that mean you could change anything?

This is your reality, no one else's

You have a choice to make, and it's a big one. You can choose now to take responsibility, or you can choose to live the life you've already got – being simply an effect of life. And if you choose to be an effect of life, fine. As much as it would sadden me, it's up to you to step up and make the change and no one else can force it. I'm honest about the fact that this process truly works. However, first you've got to take responsibility for where you are right now.

But you may be thinking, 'I didn't create this dis-ease, dis-order or psychological issue.' Perhaps not consciously, but a dis-ease of the body or a psychological issue is only formed by stress on the body. Sure, the right level of stress can be healthy for us, as it keeps us active and driven, but continuous, overwhelming stress can start to have a negative effect, throwing the body out of balance and causing our unconscious to develop symptoms or issues. How we react to situations can cause undue stress, too. The way you react causes your body – your physical body – to produce something like dis-ease or dis-order. It's your body's way of communicating with your mind and is a coping mechanism known as the fight or flight response. If you put enough pressure and strain on the communication chain, it's going to snap. If you put enough pressure on a relationship, you're going to break up. If you put enough pressure on your life, some part of your body is just going to feel like it can't cope anymore. And that's where I believe we get most of our dis-eases and dis-orders.

This is the reason why so many people suffer from depression, anxiety, fears, phobias or low self-esteem/confidence. When we experience high levels of physical or emotional stress over a prolonged period, we can develop psychological or physiological symptoms that tell us we need to pay attention to our minds and bodies in order to resolve the symptoms. The first step in resolving this conflict between body and mind is to take responsibility for our present situation.

Maggie's story

Maggie came to me suffering with low self-esteem. Her overbearing, highly critical and aggressive boss was bullying her. Over the years the bullying led her to experience very low self-esteem and anxiety in every area of her life, and caused her to suffer various stress-related health issues. She told me that she 'no longer felt worthy' or 'good enough' in life. In saying this, you can see how she 'took on' the belief system imposed by her boss. But no one can cause us to take on a belief or take on any psychological issue. At an unconscious level, Maggie's mind chose to accept the limiting belief of 'not being good enough' or 'worthless' as truth.

When she realized that she had inadvertently adopted the beliefs of her boss, she also realized that she could let them go and take ownership of her mind and body. She shifted her thinking from believing she was not good enough and a victim to realizing that she could own her mind if she took responsibility for her thoughts and present situation. Being in charge of her results, and taking back the power, opened her mind to many new and exciting possibilities.

So, by taking responsibility now, rather than letting life have an effect on you, you'll begin to see that everything around you is your creation in the most powerful way you can imagine.

Let life be a product of you

Allow life to be a product of what you want it to be. If we own the situation and take responsibility for it, we can then change it. Otherwise we just keep reaffirming where we already are, and pushing it outside our control.

Move from the 'effect' to the 'cause' side of the equation, because when you take responsibility you get results.

Results will empower you, and empowerment gives you the confidence to get anything that you want, to manifest all the things that you desire, all the successes and outcomes.

Since awakening myself to what is true, I've taken responsibility for everything I've done in the last ten years and what I do now. No matter what is in my life, I take responsibility for it. If someone is behaving badly towards me in a friendship or relationship, I take responsibility for that. I have allowed that person into my life, and I have to choose to keep them in my life or to cut them out, whether they are family or friends. It sounds quite harsh, but you've got to look after your own interests, your own wellbeing, and the people in your life should be those who only want the best for you. You've got to be healthy if you want to be your true potential.

Okay, so you may not want to cut some negative people out of your life. Guess what, though? When you change, they change. When you act on your true potential, you attract people into your life who are on the same wavelength, who are on the same 'vibration' as you. Entrepreneurs get together in groups to brainstorm because they are surrounding themselves with powerful people, people with ideas.

It gives them the energy and heightened vibrations to be able to create new ideas, too.

Unconsciously, our minds seek out people who are similar to us – ultimately, 'like' attracts 'like'. So we attract those with the same mindset more often than not because we seek out what is familiar to us. Your mindset can be comprised of the values you hold, your beliefs and your world outlook. We rarely associate with those who go against our values and worldview and, you could say, those people justify our worldview too – because *they* will rarely choose to associate with *us*.

We are made of energy, and we attract those who are of similar energy to us.

If people associate with people they don't like – or those who always put them down – of course they're going to feel let down. It's going to lower their vibration or energy and will make them feel bad.

A real way of making changes in someone else is to be the best you can be and *show* them they can change too. Ghandi once said, 'We need to be the change we want to see in the world'. By being the example of change. In the other person's reality, they see the world in a certain way, but when they see someone contradicting it in a positive way, they see that it's possible to make changes in themselves, too. They are seeing it, they are hearing it, they are experiencing it and they have to, at an unconscious level, take on the new possibility.

Aaron's story

My client Aaron had a partner who would always complain and blame others for her situation. It caused Aaron to resent his partner, and also to become negative and complain himself. One option he considered was breaking up with her because he couldn't handle her negativity anymore. However, our focus was to take on responsibility for managing our emotional state and to develop a core mindset of self-belief and positivity, and the amazing thing was that the change within Aaron was so powerful that his partner absorbed his new mindset too, and she saw that there was another way of living – positively.

So, you could take Ghandi's advice to be 'the change' you want to see in others as an example of what is possible and others will see it, but also unconsciously take it on as a way of being. You are the sum of the closest people you spend time with, which makes you wonder... who are you choosing to hang around with, and how do they affect you? Are they enabling you to grow and be happy, or do they repress you and keep you down?

If your environment and the people in your life are getting you down, it doesn't have to be that way; you can choose. People forget to tell you this, but you can choose. You have a choice. No matter what your situation is, take responsibility for it and own it like it's yours. Why? Because it *is* yours.

Choose to create your reality by taking responsibility for it.

Taking responsibility for your life is the real key to getting everything that you want, because it means you have the power to change it. Otherwise you push everything outside of you, which means you can't own it, control it or change it.

So you have to take responsibility now. Take responsibility for every aspect of your life and I can guarantee it will be so empowering that it will change your day, every day. You will feel happier and happier with each moment in the knowledge that you can choose to have the life you deserve – especially when we begin to work with your unconscious mind through hypnosis (use the free audio downloads at www.josephclough.com/byp in sequence as you go through the book). These techniques will give you the wisdom and mindset that will allow you to get those things that you want, because you can attract anything that you want into your life through the power of your thoughts and actions.

Your mind is the most powerful thing you have. It's a fact. Your mind is the most powerful tool you can ever use. We don't get a manual for our minds, but you can consciously create your own manual and use it to recalibrate your mind and body, to attract the things that you want into your life.

Your perception is your 'projection' in life

Whatever you perceive to be true is true for you. Henry Ford once said 'Whether you think you can or think you can't, you're right.' And it's an amazing saying, really, because whatever you really think about yourself – about the situations you go into, whether you think you're going to fail or succeed, whether you think relationships are good or bad, whether you think about money as 'abundance' or 'debt', a 'good thing' or a 'bad thing', whether you think it's 'easy' to get or 'hard' to get – whatever you think you are, in a sense, you are right in your model of the world. It's all about what you perceive to be true. And your perception is what you're projecting into your life right now.

Is the glass half full or half empty?

It doesn't matter, because it is whatever you perceive it to be. And it's about training your perceptions to be different, to be efficient and positive. It's about changing your level of focus.

For example, you go through a situation – it could be any event, either good or bad – and you take that event in through your five senses (your eyes, ears, touch, smell and taste). Now when you take in the event through your senses, your mind will delete, distort and generalize some of the information that you are experiencing. At any given moment we are taking in between two and four million bits of information per second (studies vary, but either way it's a lot of information). Now, if we were conscious of those two million bits per second it would overwhelm us totally. We wouldn't be able to cope with it all, so the unconscious filters the information and puts it into smaller pieces so we can comprehend the situation and understand what is going on.

In order to do that, your brain has to delete some pieces of information, and it does this on the basis of whether it thinks you need to know it or not; if something else is more important, it will delete it. For example, have you ever tried to speak to someone when they are engrossed in a TV show? You are there in their awareness, but they delete your voice as all their attention is on the screen. There is a saying that some people only ever hear what they want to hear. It's as if we delete everything else to fit our own model of the world.

Our brains also distort our experience in accordance with our beliefs and values. An extreme example of this distortion is when people have an eating disorder such as anorexia. The person will see his or her reflection in a mirror and see someone horribly overweight. But in reality, are they overweight? Well, no, quite the opposite. The sufferer can be extremely unwell and severely underweight, but their mind creates a different picture; it distorts how they perceive their reality. In the same way, your mind is capable of distorting information every day, depending on how it processes what you're receiving. The distortion can be compared to walking at nighttime. You can see something in the far distance but you're not quite sure what it is so your brain twists and turns it into possibilities... is it a person? As you get closer, your vision gets clearer, and you see that it's perhaps just a small tree or shrub that looked like a person.

We generalize about things, too. Throughout our day we generalize about events and situations because of past experiences. Let me break this down a little. If someone has a bad relationship ten times in a row, they're likely to think the next one's going to be bad too, or that all men are bad or all women are bad. If previous job interviews haven't gone well, it can cause us to project those experiences into the next one and cause us to feel anxious and to think it won't go well.

But in thinking this way, we're literally taking those past experiences and projecting them onto the next situation. If you have a bad situation at work, it may scare you and make you want to avoid doing it again because you're generalizing that every future experience is going to be more of the same.

We also have national, cultural and global generalizations. For example, you may think it's true (if you're a woman) that men can't multitask, and (if you're a man) that women can't drive; both are generalizations. We also blow things out of proportion, for example saying that our whole day was a disaster when perhaps something went wrong in the evening, and because that's all we remember, we distort the impact of the situation and delete the things that went well.

Generalizations can also be limiting beliefs about wealth and abundance, such as, 'money doesn't grow on trees', or it's 'the root of all evil' and 'no pain, no gain'. I'm sorry, but to me that is just rubbish. Do you think successful entrepreneurs had beliefs like that before they got their millions? No, they didn't. They thought, 'I deserve to get this and I'm going to get it, no matter what'.

So, the mind deletes information that it doesn't think is necessary; it distorts information and also generalizes situations. Our minds will do this for certain reasons that we believe serve us, and in accordance with the beliefs that we hold. So, any external situation will be experienced by your five senses, and your beliefs can change how you perceive it.

Joe's story

I remember seeing a client many years ago called Joe who declared, 'I'm just not good enough to get a job. Everyone else thinks I am good enough, and I'm always offered promotions, but I don't think I'm good enough so I'm not going to go for that opportunity – I'm going to be found out one day for being the failure that I really am.' His beliefs about himself changed the way he saw opportunities in life and he didn't go for jobs, didn't go into the relationships he wanted and wasn't able to make the changes he desired. When we removed his beliefs he clearly saw his potential – how 'good' he was – and, because of that, he saw a whole new world of opportunities to explore and so changed his outcome.

Beliefs can distort and generalize how we see our reality.

Memories

Then there are our past memories. If you have had a number of bad experiences, you're likely to think that the next experience is going to be bad too. And if we flip that over, the more good experiences you have in that situation, the more you tend to expect and think it's going to be equally good or even better.

So our memories and our beliefs have a massive impact on how we perceive our reality, as do our values. If you place a high value on money, you're going to go and find opportunities to make money. If you place a lower value on money, or you associate money as being the 'root of all evil' or ' hard to get', then you're less likely to be on the lookout for those moneymaking opportunities.

The values that you were brought up with as a child – inherited from your parents, family and teachers, and adopted from your peers – have an effect on how you perceive your life and your reality, as well as your current attitudes.

The people who have the most optimistic attitude are the happiest people around. They see life, opportunity and happiness in everything that they do. They look out for those situations and attract them into their life by the very thoughts they have in their minds. But those who are pessimistic will see doom and gloom. Whatever your current outlook, you can retrain your mind to project and attract the future you really deserve.

Then there are the decisions that we make. You could make a decision as a child, or a year ago, or even just a few moments ago, to get your life the way that you want it. That decision changes your perception of life. You think, 'Yeah, I'm going to go for it. I'm going to seek out opportunities.' But if you've made the decision in the past that you're not 'good enough' or that you're 'not worthy' of getting the life that you want – not to worry, we'll soon change that – it's going to affect how you see your life, your choices and your opportunities.

There are also the decisions that we make about our health at an unconscious level: the decision to be unhappy or to feel depressed, the decision about how to react to certain situations, to have phobias and anxiety attacks, the decision to have dis-ease or dis-orders. The decisions we make change the way we perceive our reality. Therefore, if we always look out and see one way or the other, we're going to attract that thing into our life.

It's interesting to note that when some people are diagnosed with cancer they decide it means the end of the world and death, while others take the diagnosis as a wakeup call, to take perspective and experience new things. For them, you could say that cancer means life rather than death, and it persuades them to live life fully.

If children have the ability to ignore all odds and percentages, then maybe we can all learn from them. When you think about it, what other choice is there but to hope? We have two options, medically and emotionally: give up, or Fight Like Hell.

Whatever you focus on, you bring about

The brain has a reticular activating system that searches for information. In other words, if you have a continuous thought, or a certain mindset, it will seek out those answers whether they are good or bad. That is why when there's a car you really want, you see it everywhere, or when you learn a new word you see it popping up everywhere. You are looking out for that piece of information. The body and mind try to draw out those opportunities to see or have that thing.

However, if you perceive negative things – if you see all the things you're going to fail at, all the things you're not good enough to get, all the poor relationships, all the bad health you're going to get and all the reasons and excuses you may have – the reticular activating system will literally search for those outcomes too. It will focus on those negative perceptions. Whatever you're focusing on, you bring about.

But we can flip that over. If you truly believe you're good enough and worthy in every situation – whether it's money, your health, relationships or career – then your brain will begin to look out for that information, for example, seeking out opportunities to find the right person in your life and truly attract them. It will find those situations in your career that will enable you to progress and live your life, and your career, in all the abundance that you deserve.

If you feel positive about your health, your mind and body will regenerate themselves to get to where you want to be – and you'll enjoy good health. So your focus is very important. If you focus on negative things, you're going to think more about negative things and therefore feel negative emotions too. People who are really anxious about a situation create images in their minds about all the things that will go wrong, which in turn causes their bodies to feel panicky and anxious, and fearful of doing that thing. So when they go into that situation, they completely fail and reaffirm their fears because they imagined it already, or they simply avoid that situation again due to overwhelming anxiety.

The most powerful thing you have is your mind, and you can focus your mind on the things that you want to achieve rather than the things that you don't want to. It's about retraining your mind and taking control of the results that you're producing.

Think of your mind as being like a Satnav. When we plan our journey, and we put our destination into the Satnav, that intelligent piece of equipment is able to plan the best route. But what if we had to put in every destination we *didn't* want to go to first? We would be taken to all the places we didn't want to go to and never get to our true destination. Sounds ridiculous, doesn't it? So why do we do it with our brains? After all, our brains are a lot more intelligent than a Satnav: we think about what we want and our brains seek the answer. If your thoughts are focused on the negative, your brain will find more of the negative in your experience; but if you focus on what you want in the positive, your brain will seek more of the positive, too.

It's time to wake up and become conscious of your thoughts.

Interpreting events

So, we take that one event, whether it is good or bad, and we take it in through our five senses. We then delete, distort and generalize the things we're taking in with regards to our beliefs, our attitudes, our memories, our values and our decisions. We then make an image in our minds of what we think we're seeing. That external event will be completely different because our eyes don't see what's really out there in the world. The eyes just take in the information. We create the image of what we think is true and then we see what we want to see. And when we make that image in our minds of what we think is happening out there, our bodies feel and react in a certain way.

So, if someone goes through a situation and has a negative perspective of it – maybe because they have limiting beliefs or traumatic memories, or have made poor decisions in the past – this will result in their body feeling bad or 'low'. But if they think positively about that situation – with a great attitude, great beliefs and values – then they begin to create new associations to their memories and all their future memories, and their body therefore changes. Their whole physiology changes, so their mind and body produces a different outcome, a different result.

And you've got to get each one of those perceptions or thoughts in alignment in order to gain your required outcome, to generate the most amazing beliefs, to have the most wonderful values, to make empowering decisions that actually give you more freedom and opportunities, to truly manifest the things that you want in life.

It's only through your brain's ability to translate vibrations that you're able to understand the world around you, your reality. So, in other words, through your eyes you translate light waves into vibrations or pictures. Your ears translate the vibrations of all the sounds. Your tongue, nose and fingertips translate the vibrations into tastes, smells and touches. All of this information helps you understand the world around you, and then you make a decision – you decide on a way of perceiving how you want the world to be, whether it is negative or positive.

We are the creators of our reality

Whatever you perceive right now, you're projecting it into your reality. You're literally attracting it into your life at some level. The feelings that we have inside, the real emotions that we're having, are the judges of what we're getting. Because as we're taking those vibrations in, they are making us vibrate. If we're really happy, we're vibrating really strongly. We feel full of energy. Like a frequency, we attract the 'like' back to us. Some people call it the law of attraction, but I see it like this: if you think in the way that you want to, you think positively – your mind and body will produce the results you need to achieve your dreams.

This is because we're fundamentally interconnected with everything around us. Everything around us is pure energy. Now, if we're pure energy – if you take our atoms down to the smallest form, we're just vibrating energy, and so is everything around us – then our thoughts are also 'vibrating' energy. If those thoughts are vibrating at a 'lower' frequency, we're going to attract low-frequency things. We're going to attract the things that we don't really want. But if we have empowering, positive thoughts, beliefs and perceptions, we're going to start to project and attract the positive back to us. We're going to find the equal opposite to get what we really want. It's all about changing your focus.

You have more potential than you think.
You are always more than you think.

If we take responsibility for all the situations that we are in right now in the most empowering way, for everything in our lives, and begin to own them and control them, we can begin to attract more and take on new perceptions. If we gain control of our minds (which we'll be doing in the next few chapters), if we gain control of our perceptions, we're going to start to project the reality that we deserve and therefore attract it into manifestation.

Gratitude for life

First, I've got a task for you. I've got a process that I want you to do for the next 15 minutes. This process is about changing your focus. It's about having gratitude for your life, because if you feel an 'attitude of gratitude', you're going to shift your focus onto the good things that you already have. You're going to shift the way that you think, and therefore you're going to start to attract the things that you want, to be your potential, so your mind and body can truly have gratitude for life.

I want you to create – either in a notepad or on your computer – a 'Journal Of Gratitude' and write down all the things that you appreciate in your life. (You can download a Journal of Gratitude PDF from my website, www.josephclough.com/byp.) And if you are thinking, 'But I don't like *anything* in my life', change your perception because there is always something! You can appreciate that you've made the decision to read this book and get your life back in order. You can appreciate that you have clothes that you're wearing right now. You can appreciate that you have a house or a roof over your head. You can appreciate that you have some family and friends. You can have the appreciation that you're able to read this book with your eyes. You can have appreciation for the natural world, if you really think about all the beauty out there. You can appreciate so many things if you change your focus. The power of focus is amazing in getting your results.

So, for the next seven days – and, ideally, every week after that – write down everything that makes you feel gratitude. Start your list by writing the words: 'I am truly grateful for the following in my life...' I want this to become a habit inside of you, to write down ten things that you appreciate every morning – even if they're the same things every day. When you start appreciating them, and getting the feeling of gratitude as you're writing them down, really being thankful that you have them in your life, then your mind and body will begin to shift their perception throughout the rest of the day, searching for more things to appreciate and attract into your life. So go ahead right now and start that process. Write down ten things (or more) that you really appreciate and have gratitude for.

Recap

- It's time to step up, to want more and be more. To be our potential.

- We must give up our limitations and make the choice to no longer 'buy into' the reasons why we are like we are. When we do this, we change our focus from scarcity and lack to infinite possibilities of potential.

- Our present situation is governed by our past actions and decisions, but our future is governed by what we do now in the present – it all starts right now!

- When we no longer give into the reasons and excuses as to why we are like we are, we reclaim ownership of our minds, bodies and souls, and have the power to make transformational changes to them. We do this by taking responsibility for our lives.

- Rather than being a product of life, allow life to be a product of what you choose to be.

- Results largely come from our perception of life: when we change our focus to what we desire, while focusing on what we are grateful for, our perception of life changes and our unconscious mind seeks and attracts the opportunities to achieve our desires.

Be Your Potential.

CHAPTER TWO

THE POWER OF FOCUS

We need to take responsibility for our lives, to be the cause of our lives and therefore take charge of all the things that we do and all the things that happen in our reality. Hopefully you have written down at least ten things that you have gratitude for at the end of the last chapter (if not, DO IT!).

So, now it is time to learn about how your reality is constructed, and how you can tap into your potential in a way that is easy and efficient in producing the results that you want. I fully understand that where you are right now is due to your past results, whether that's due to your attitudes, your beliefs, your values or even the decisions you've made in the past. But one of the things that makes this book different from others is that we are going to be working with the unconscious mind – your unconscious mind.

The unconscious – the gateway to excellence

But first of all, what is the unconscious mind? The way I see it, if you had conscious control over where you are right now, if you had conscious control over the limiting beliefs, thoughts or processes you run, or even your behaviours that aren't producing the results you desire, you would simply change them, wouldn't you?

But if we don't have that control, if we don't have the ability to simply change our behaviours or change our minds and therefore our results, it must mean they're being run at an unconscious level.

If you can change your unconscious mind, you can change those beliefs, attitudes and perceptions, and even the decisions you've made in the past. So it's important to be able to reprogramme the way the mind works, and we can do that directly by working with the unconscious. For example, in NLP there is a powerful tool called 'reframing', which means changing our perception or point of view about an experience. This process alone can have a major influence on how you perceive, interpret and react to that experience, or even your past experiences. For example, I have worked with people who have had the absolute belief that 'cancer will cause them to die' – it's simply the conclusion and outcome they perceive to be true at that moment. Is this mindset or belief a true or healthy perception to have? Of course not, so to reframe their perception of their health, we can ask them questions that cause them to have a different perception of life, for example:

'Do you know of any other people who had cancer yet survived or went into remission?'

'What if all the scientists looking for the cure for cancer had that belief system?'

'Would you want your children to have that belief system?'

'Or maybe, just maybe, there have been people in the world who were diagnosed with cancer and it led them to actually start living with the full knowledge of how precious life is?'

Could those people with the belief that 'cancer will cause them to die' still hold that belief as an *absolute truth* after considering these questions? I very much doubt they could, because of the new insight that cancer does not always mean death. Therefore we break the limiting belief. Looking for alternative viewpoints gives us new perceptions on how we see the world. It takes us from a closed mind with no options to one where we are looking for new possibilities, teachings and potential.

And when I said that our minds are the most powerful tools that we actually have and ever will have, I meant the unconscious part of our minds. Because if you can gain control of your unconscious, you will be able to change the results that you're getting to the ones that you want.

Your unconscious mind runs processes like the 'fight or flight' response. It also maintains your whole body. It runs all the vital organs and processes, such as breathing, as well as fighting off disease and healing the body. So when you become ill, your unconscious mind assumes control and works on returning you to good health. It also maintains all the skills we've learned in the past, too. Because, if you think about it, for those who know how to drive a car – or even ride a bike – when you first learned you were probably consciously overwhelmed by the whole idea of mastering control and operating the car. You were consciously thinking about having to work the gears, the clutch, checking the mirrors, the speedometer and so on, as well as focusing on what was happening outside the vehicle. But after a while, once you had done the behaviour once, twice or 50 times, your mind began to run that behaviour at an unconscious level, and that's when it became second nature – unconscious.

Before we truly learn something as a way of being, we are 'consciously incompetent'. In other words, we have no idea what or how to do something when learning a new skill or behaviour. But as we start to learn, we begin to know the steps consciously, and as we continue to practise them we become 'consciously competent' in that skill or behaviour. When we do that skill or behaviour a set amount of times, our unconscious mind learns the process too, making it a habit that becomes second nature to us. As a result, this skill or behaviour can be run without our conscious involvement because we have become 'unconsciously competent'.

And the same is true of everything we do. When you see a young child learning to walk, they're very conscious of what they're doing. They consciously try to push themselves up and move their legs in the way that adults do. They're literally modelling and copying how adults walk. And sometimes they fall down because they're just not used to it yet. They are consciously and unconsciously incompetent at the beginning – they don't have that level of control or coordination. But after a while it becomes natural to them, and very quickly they're able to walk very efficiently and less like an out-of-sync robot.

The same is true of every habit you've ever produced. The behaviours become natural to you. This also goes for the beliefs you hold. If you have the thought that you're 'not good enough' and you keep on thinking that way, feeling 'not good enough' over a period of time, it will become cemented and ingrained into your unconscious mind so you believe you're 'not good enough', or you're 'not worthy' or you 'can't' have the relationships and money or health that you deserve.

Through repetition, habits become solidified inside our neurology and our mindset is programmed to be able to carry out certain behaviours. But guess what? If you flip that around and keep on thinking, perceiving, acting and reacting from a state of potential and excellence, your mind will allow that to become a habit, even if you don't feel that way at first.

As I mentioned earlier in the book, I was once a chronic blusher. I blushed so many times for so many years that it became an ingrained habit and a part of my identity, so much so that I believed it would never go and that it was simply a part of who I was. But when I realized that it was my mental and physical body triggering it in certain situations, I used the mindsets and processes I'm sharing in this book to reprogramme my mind to interrupt the habit and win confidence in any situation. Imagine an overgrown garden. If we were to go down one route in it repeatedly over a period of time, there would be a well-trodden pathway set out before us. It would be quite easy to walk down that route every time we crossed the garden. Now let's make the garden the mind: the more we go down one particular way of thinking, the more it becomes a way of being, a habit. When we decide to take a new path (a new way of thinking), it causes us to develop a new pathway to a new destination that we desire. If we focus on that new way of thinking and feeling it will quickly become a new habit, but an empowering one that we have chosen to take on. For me personally, in time, the new pathway had a profound effect on my life – I went from blushing and feeling anxious to being free to live my life, being confident and calm in any situation.

Allow your focus to expand on how you would like to think, feel and behave, and very quickly you'll develop new, safer habits that are also empowering and full of freedom to be how you choose to be. Through repetition, they will eventually become cemented as part of your identity, the core of your being, your potential. Those new, ingrained, empowering beliefs will then attract all the perfect relationships, the abundance of money, the absolute contentment to your life and will enable you to begin to generate wellbeing.

So, the unconscious mind does try to do the most amazing things for us and it's always trying to help us. It's always trying to do the best for us by keeping us safe – by maintaining and running our bodies – and generating habits so we have to pay less attention to them consciously.

Why does the unconscious run poor beliefs, attitudes and behaviours?

But you may be thinking, 'Why does the unconscious run things such as depression, fears and phobias, and these limiting beliefs about producing the perfect relationship?' Or, 'Why can't I stop my limiting attitudes, thoughts or beliefs consciously, rather my unconscious mind running them?'

No matter what behaviours you're running right now, no matter what beliefs or mindsets, no matter what results you're producing, your unconscious mind is doing it with the best of intentions. It's always trying to help you. Unfortunately, the behaviours it produces do not always match its highest intention. Let's take a few examples that illustrate how the unconscious mind's intentions are good.

If someone has a phobia, whether it is of spiders, planes, lifts or anything, what's the intention of the unconscious for that person? The behaviour provokes an overwhelming fear of something, or a situation, and that's the behaviour (the outcome), but what's it really *trying* to do for that person? What's the intention? Well, by running an extreme version of the fight or flight response, it's trying to protect that person from the feared thing. Although the intention is good, the intention of protection is producing an extreme behaviour – an overwhelming fear that is actually damaging the body. Ironically, the mind is probably causing more stress and strain than the feared thing itself could do. It has generalized and distorted that thing into 'I hate it, it's going to hurt me' at an unconscious level. It's a great intention, but the behaviour is not helpful and produces a negative outcome – fear and panic attacks.

Let's say someone experiences low self-esteem. Why do the mind and body produce thoughts and beliefs like 'I'm not good enough'? Well, most of time it's because that belief system stops us from going into situations that might harm us, or where we might fail: 'If I'm not good enough, I won't try new things in case I fail/look silly/get hurt'. So limiting belief/low self-esteem is a horrible condition to experience, but it has the greatest of intention for us – a protection mechanism that makes us stay in our comfort zones and remain safe.

What about the belief that 'all men/women will use and abuse me'? Again, the behaviour is trying to protect you. If you've had a certain number of bad relationships, you're going to generalize that all men or women are exactly like that. So when you go into a situation or a relationship, your unconscious mind is saying, 'this person is going to abuse me' because it's going by its past experiences. However, the protection the mind creates backfires, as it is likely to attract the exact same problems into your life – more pain and more anguish in relationships.

What about anxiety? Why would we want to create images and feelings inside us of all the bad things that might happen, or all the things that might go wrong? The unconscious intention is to stop us from going into that situation, or to plan for all the bad things that 'might' happen, so we know how to react. But unfortunately it does it in such an overwhelming way that we become over-anxious in the situation – no matter what happens – rather than just prior to it.

So, although your unconscious mind tries to do good things – the intention is always positive – the behaviours it produces can be terrible, and don't get the results needed.

Good news

We've discovered that whatever you're doing right now, your mind is doing it for a positive purpose. It's trying to do it with the best of intentions. This *is* good news, because if it's trying to help us, we can give it a more efficient way of producing that result – a healthier, safer way that really allows us to produce the results we deserve.

I can tell you now, your unconscious mind would jump at that chance; it would want to grasp it at every opportunity. And it's better than your unconscious mind wanting to do it for bad reasons, or to actually go against you. That just isn't possible; your unconscious mind is always trying to do something good for you. So, we can literally work with the unconscious mind to retrain it, and to cultivate it to get into alignment with you and your outcomes. This is one of the big issues in life – you say on the one hand, 'I want to be happy, I want to have the perfect relationship with my soul mate', or 'I want to have a career I'm passionate about', or 'I want health and vitality in my life', or 'I want financial abundance'. But on the other hand, there's a part of you that may be thinking. 'but I'm not good enough for that', or 'I don't have the ability to achieve that finance', or 'all men/women are just bad news, they're just going to cause me more pain', or 'money is a bad thing, it just has bad attachments and associations' or 'you've got to work really hard to get it'.

Perhaps you have values that are incongruent in getting your results. Or maybe you have extreme feelings – like anger, sadness, fear, hurt, guilt, frustration and so on – so no matter how much you want it, there's a part of you that is just not getting you there. And when you get that conflict, that's where the issue arises and you feel conflict within yourself. What we want to do is get those two parts together now, to negotiate a new way of being and develop new behaviours, new perceptions, new beliefs and resources that will allow you to be truly aligned in getting your outcome.

I know for a fact that if you are 100 per cent aligned to getting your outcome, which you're focusing on at a conscious and unconscious level, you will get your results – you can't fail to succeed. It's only doubts, fears, limiting beliefs, limiting thoughts and bad behaviours stopping you from achieving it. And that's where your internal conflicts arise. If you're completely aligned, you're completely contented and you're completely congruent in getting your results. And that's where we're heading now; we're heading to get that alignment in whatever the outcome is for you. That's one of the reasons why I set the task of having the attitude of gratitude, because you're changing your level of focus, you're getting 100 per cent of you to focus on what is good in your life and therefore focusing on getting more of it.

We can become aligned and congruent by becoming conscious and reconnecting with ourselves. I personally think we have conflicts because we are out of alignment and out of rapport with our unconscious. If we are incongruent with our desires, we may unconsciously self-sabotage.

Sebastian's story
One of my clients did exactly that. Sebastian wanted to expand his business consciously, but

deep down, he thought he was unworthy of such success, so he continued to self-sabotage with procrastination, missing meetings and shying away from opportunities by generating excuses. When he became conscious of his self-sabotaging ways, it opened up the connection with his unconscious mind to realize his own self-worth, and how grateful he was for who he was. It was an awakening and it aligned him with his true desires and self-worth.

When someone lives congruently they act in accordance with their desires, dreams and goals in the knowledge that it is their path, despite any influence from others. Were Ghandi, Martin Luther King and Mother Teresa aligned with their actions? Yes, they were! They may not have known how to do what they did, but they knew it was right; they knew their path, despite obstacles that came their way.

When we are grateful for what we have, we shift our attention from scarcity and fear to gratitude, joy, optimism and possibility, which causes us to be in alignment with our desires from the inside out.

So everything that you're producing right now, you can be thankful for and appreciate your mind and body for having the best of intentions. And then it's just about rekindling your communication with your unconscious mind to manifest the results that you want. Results that are aligned with positive intentions will now far outweigh your present behaviours and results.

Everything your unconscious mind is doing, it's doing with a positive intention – this is a valuable key.

Dealing with the past

Your unconscious mind also stores memories and past experiences for you, and it does this for positive purposes once again – so you know about future situations. Your mind is literally judging your future by looking back at the past, on a conscious or unconscious level. So, if you had a bad experience 'X' number of times, when you go into a future experience, or a present experience, you're going to have to remember those in order to see what that situation may hold for you.

So, if we had lots of anger in the past, lots of fear, lots of guilt, hurt and frustration, or made lots of limiting decisions, we're likely to have negative mindsets and therefore perceive negative things in our future. Our focus is in the wrong lane again. However, if we clean up those memories, release all the negative unwarranted emotions and limiting decisions, we literally have a clean past, and when we go into a future situation, we have all the learning we require without any of the negative feelings associated with the memories.

The unconscious is also the domain of your emotions. You're not completely in control of your emotions – that's why you have fears and anxieties about things – which is why you can hold hurt, guilt or sadness for many years. But you can communicate with your unconscious mind *now* and begin to let go of those negative emotions and preserve positive insights and teachings that will keep you safe, rather than having the fear, anger, hurt, sadness or guilt.

The unconscious mind runs your body and it has a blueprint of what's happening in your body right now. It knows your health, it knows the balance of what you're doing, how you are right now. It's always eavesdropping on what you're thinking. That is why, when people are depressed, their bodies get depressed too, and they suffer from low energy and lethargy. But for those who are happy, the body responds in an energetic and vibrant way. So your body always knows where you are right now, and it's learning and listening from whatever you're thinking and feeling.

I believe our DNA has all the information it needs to be able to produce the perfect health, but unfortunately, holding onto limiting decisions or negative emotions has an effect on how our bodies respond and therefore causes stress and strain, which can break the chain of good health. However, when we get in control of our minds and tap into our potential – our source energy – we can tap into that perfect blueprint for the perfect health.

So your unconscious focus will always be trying to preserve and protect you, while maintaining the integrity of your body. It enjoys serving you but it needs clear orders to follow. This means if you're constantly thinking about all the negative things, all the bad things that may happen and are focused on negative associations or the 'lack of', you're going to send that signal throughout your body by those very images that you're creating and holding in your mind – your thoughts.

Changing focus

So, we need to change our focus. We need to focus on what we want, giving clear orders to our unconscious minds to have the perfect health – to attract the perfect relationships, to retrain our minds to think clearly and abundantly in every way.

It doesn't happen overnight – although it can for some people, so watch out for those results – but usually it needs repetition. Your body has been programmed to get your present results. Like learning to ride a bike, or how to walk, or how to drive, it needs repetition to become unconscious.

This is where the task at the end of Chapter 1 will really help you to assume that mindset and *attitude of gratitude* every morning. Because feeling positive about what you *do* have will soon become a habit, and your mind and body will automatically start thinking like that too – automatically searching for the positive results you deserve.

When you keep thinking of what you want – directing your focus towards where you want to be – that too will become a habit. It will become unconscious, it will become a residual behaviour inside of you that will automatically produce the results that you deserve and desire. So this repetition will generate the results that you want.

I've designed these processes to work on your unconscious mind, and they will work much quicker than you can consciously, so to install new habits of success, go to www.josephclough.com/byp and download or listen to the *Power of Focus* hypnosis track.

The unconscious mind also functions best as a whole integrated unit. If there's doubt or fear creating conflict within you, it means that you're torn between getting your outcome and the outcome never being achieved. However, when you're 100 per cent congruent, 100 per cent aligned, and your whole body – your whole conscious and unconscious mind is functioning as a whole, integrated unit – you will get the results that you want and truly deserve in every way.

It's only when our bodies are in dis-order, in conflict or in dis-ease that they produce and manifest the things that we don't like. They could manifest poor health, such as dis-ease or dis-order, the stress and strain breaking the chain of great health. Or maybe produce conflicting negative thoughts, attitudes and beliefs, or negative overwhelming emotions. However, when we get true congruent alignment, when we're being our potential, we get results. That is when we truly manifest and attract those people, those situations, money and health – that perfect reality – into our lives.

The unconscious mind is also attuned to symbols. By this I mean that everything you see around you, you've literally labelled in some way and it's a symbol for you. If you're sitting on.a chair, you know that it is a 'chair' – the word 'chair' is a symbol – and you know what it means and how to use it because you've given it a meaning. Our whole language is made up of symbols. A red traffic light is a symbol to stop, while green means go. Hearing the telephone ring is a signal to listen and respond. Everything is a symbol, and your unconscious mind thrives on responding to symbols. So it does a great job in making sense of the world around you by labelling and giving meaning to everything.

But unfortunately, if you're holding negative thoughts, negative feelings or negative internal representations, your body begins to think that way too – it's literally receives those thoughts, feelings and internal representations and then produces those same results. However, if you produce the most wonderful thoughts inside your mind, the most wonderful images and feelings and emotions inside of you, your unconscious mind begins to attract that into your life.

The unconscious also takes everything personally. Everything that you perceive in your reality right now – all the results that you're getting – is down to how your mind filters your beliefs, attitudes, memories and values. Even your thoughts, the very images you're holding in your mind right now. This means that if you're talking to yourself in a negative way, or if you're thinking in a negative way and beating yourself up, or if talking yourself down, then your body is going to take that personally. I know for a fact that when people feel extremely guilty, or they feel really hurt, stressed or sad, their bodies become conflicted and they feel hurt too.

The mind–body communication is always there, completely interconnected.

So we've got to perceive our lives and ourselves in a new way. We've got to start building ourselves up, remembering our true potential, remembering that life is meant to be good, remembering that we're really loved – remembering that we are our reality and we are the creators here, no one else.

So how can we stop negative thoughts?

To stop negative thoughts we must first become conscious of them. Usually we allow negative thoughts to send our thinking on a tangent. With each one we allow to happen, more are bred. Think of your negative thoughts as being like a snowball rolling down a hill, building up in force and size. Before you know it, you are being overrun by negative thoughts. You are the controller of your thoughts, and as soon as you catch yourself thinking negatively, it's your signal to focus on what you want. Very much like how if you start to feel anxious, it's your signal to focus on what you need to do and change the course of direction. We know now that whatever we perceive to be true *is* true, and negative thoughts will affect how we see and perceive life. As soon as the negative thoughts pop up into your awareness, it is time to stop for a moment and focus on your desires.

You can do this in a few ways, as thoughts are sometimes tricky to conquer by positive thoughts alone. You can turn to your feelings instead, as feelings will dictate and direct your thoughts. You can literally say 'STOP!' and then put your attention to what you are grateful for. When you do this, it changes your emotional state of mind and this in turn interrupts the pattern of negative thinking.

Another way to focus on what you want is to make it part of your mindset and mantra to make any negative thinking a signal to start focusing on what you want. Think about it this way: every negative thought has a boundary, which means that every negative thought has its polar opposite thought. So, when a negative thought pops into your mind, fully consider what the opposite of that negative thought is. For example, a thought that could pop up is, 'I'm not good enough' and that's your signal to focus on counter-examples of everything you 'are good enough' at doing. This not only reverses the negative thinking, but also starts your brain looking for resources in other areas of your life that counter the thought that you are 'not good enough'. This method of thinking is very powerful and it takes you from closed thinking to positive open thinking.

Living in the 'now'

The most powerful way, however, of freeing yourself of negative thinking is by making the decision to live in the 'now'. Negative thinking relates to your past experiences and your fears for the future. When we feel 'not good enough' our minds wander back through our past memories looking for examples and reasons to confirm that thought as true. They also consider everything you want to avoid happening in the future, and this causes anxiety, fear and worry. However, when we put our attention and intention on the *now* – this present moment – we break free of the past and future thinking as all our energy is on all the potential of this moment, which is unlimited. It can be a little tricky to do this at first – as you are accustomed to negative past and future thinking – but as you become familiar with 'putting your attention on the present', you'll find that when a negative thought pops up, you focus on the now and break free of the restrictive negative thoughts.

Karl's story

One of my clients was experiencing severe anxiety on a daily basis, and had been for the previous two years. The source of his anxiety was that he was continually thinking negatively about what *might* happen to him for most of the day. In order to overcome these habitual and self-destructive thoughts, I taught him the following simple process. Whenever Karl got anxious or thought negatively, it would be his signal to simply put his attention on his breathing and just *be* in the moment and experience the joy of it, which allowed him to become grounded and strong. Knowing that negative thinking is past- and future-based thinking meant he wasn't living in the 'present', but when he learned to shift his attention to his breathing he broke free of that negative cycle.

Breathing is this moment and when our attention is on it, we give up our attention to the present. Regular practise of this simple technique enabled Karl to break free of his negative thinking and anxiety for good.

When we become conscious of our thoughts and then change their direction by focusing on what we are grateful for, and the present moment, we develop a new habit. Like the metaphor of the overgrown garden, we develop a new pathway to go down in the mind and the more we do it, the more natural and unconscious this new way of positive thinking becomes.

When you send that signal throughout your whole body you begin to produce those magical results. When you simply become the real you – the you that you've always wanted to be, the you you've always known you were but unfortunately never acted or felt that way as such – that is when you attract your perfect life.

Finally, it's worth realizing that your unconscious mind doesn't process negatives, because whatever anyone says to you now, you've got to process it. For example, if I say 'don't think of a blue tree' you've got to create an image in your mind of a 'blue tree' in order to know what *not* to think about – that's if you can do it! So, if your mind is always thinking in a negative way – and you're creating images and feelings of all the things you don't want in your life – it's going to take that as reality.

The mind can't distinguish between what is imagined and what is real

Your mind is powerful, but it needs to be guided and you are the guide. To achieve the life you desire, inwardly and outwardly, you must hold your desires firmly in your mind. Due to the mind–body connection, your mind causes your body to fall in sync with your desires, too. In other words, your unconscious mind can't tell the difference between what is imagined and what is real.

At Harvard Medical School, neuroscientist Alvaro Pascual-Leone led an experiment involving two groups of students. The first group was asked to play a simple combination of notes on the piano for two hours a day for five days. The second group did the same exercise, but instead of playing their music on a piano, they were told to just imagine their fingers playing the same simple combination of notes for two hours a day. Brain scans showed that the area of the brain connected to the finger muscles had actually grown like a muscle in *both* groups of students.

Dr David Hamilton, bestselling author and avid researcher on the mind–body connection, said, 'Your brain cannot tell the difference between something that's real and whether you are just imagining it.' So if the mind can't distinguish between what is imagined and what is real, when you think of all the things you don't want, you then have all the negative feelings with it too. This is why, when people have a fear or a phobia of something, they may even see a picture of the thing, or simply think about it in their minds. Even though they know it's not there in reality, their bodies still have the fear and anxiety there. They just can't tell the difference. As Albert Einstein noted, 'Your imagination is your preview of life's coming attractions.'

Use your mind to visualize all the things you do want, while having strong, powerful emotions in attracting it – i.e. the most powerful feelings of abundance, gratitude, love, happiness even belief in knowing that you're going to achieve those goals – that's when your body begins to actually attract it into your life, because it thinks it's true and searches for it.

Many successful people had the image of what they wanted and kept on thinking about their specific outcome. It made them aligned. It got their minds searching for the answer, seeking out those opportunities and manifesting it into their lives. You could have the most amazing ability in the world, but if you allowed your thoughts and feelings to reflect doubt and failure, you would produce those results. This is true in all areas in life but it is seen quite markedly among professional sportsmen and women. There have been a number of cases of professional athletes losing form, not because their ability changed, but because their psychological mindset had changed. Athletes that use positive visualization to imagine themselves performing well and winning greatly benefit from the practice and – like the students who imagined playing the piano – the positive visualization has a direct effect on their actual physical performance too.

Camille Duvall

The five-time World Champion and Hall of Fame water-ski champion said: 'I train myself mentally with visualization. The morning of a tournament, before I put my feet on the floor, I visualize myself making perfect runs with emphasis on technique, all the way through to what my personal best is in practice... The more you work with this type of visualization, especially when you do it on a day-to-day basis, you'll actually begin to feel your muscles contracting at the appropriate times'.

To me, positive visualization is one of the most powerful tools. Holding the image in your mind of what you really want, obsessing over it in a most positive way so that you know it's going to happen. Doing this gives you 100 per cent belief throughout your whole mind that you know it's going to happen.

When you become connected with your source, you connect to your true potential.

Your mind needs direction and the right focus from you to be able to get the outcomes you desire.

One of the most powerful ways to direct and focus your mind is by paying attention and being conscious of your feelings and emotions. The emotions that we have inside of us – the feelings we feel on a day-to-day basis – are like our guidance system. They guide us to where we want to be. If you have feelings of gratitude, love, belief and perhaps *knowing* that you're going to achieve these outcomes, it will begin to attract those things into your life. Because every thought is just energy, everything that you think right now is a vibrating wave of energy, and every thought is a signal and each one brings you back the equivalent.

Tuning in

Think of your thoughts as like radio waves. When you switch on the radio to your favourite station, you tune in at the right frequency, and get the station by matching the required frequency – you adjust the dial to the frequency you want. However, you would never ever expect to get that station if you were tuned in to a different frequency. You don't expect to hear the frequency of 98.8FM when you're tuned in to the frequency of 105.7FM, do you? Your mind is literally a frequency and your thoughts are a certain frequency. Now, if you're consistently tuned in to what you want for a period of time, it eventually gets attracted to you – you're literally sending a signal out throughout the whole of your reality.

So allow yourself to think of yourself as a frequency and, as you think of yourself as a frequency, what are you tuning in to? Are you tuning in to poor health? Are your thoughts and your feelings focused on poor health? Are they focused on another bad relationship? Are they focused on the job you don't want? Are you focusing on and feeling bad debt? Are you focusing on the lack of, or all the abundance of what you do want?

Because when you consistently put your thoughts and your feelings into the frequency of what you *do* want, you're generating that habit at a conscious and unconscious level, and it will begin to be manifested into your reality. Wherever your attention or your intention are going right now, that is where the energy is flowing to – your focus.

Are you flowing energy into what you *don't* want or what you *do* want? If your attention and thoughts run along the lines of 'I'm in debt', 'I'm not good enough', 'I am poor', 'I have bad relationships', 'I am a bad person', 'I can't get the career that I want', or 'I have this dis-ease or dis-order and it's going to kill me', then you're attracting 'alike energy' of being in debt, not being good enough, being poor, having bad relationships and living up to the expectation of death.

Are you tuning in to what you're receiving, or wanting to have? Or are you tuning in to what you don't want to have? And how can you know what you're attracting?

Be conscious of what you're attracting

Being conscious is very simple. It's about paying attention to your feelings. Paying attention to what you're feeling in each moment. Putting you in a state of gratitude, love and wellbeing. Putting you in that feeling of harmony, belief and abundance.

You may have to pretend for a while, because if you've had these limiting beliefs or negative feelings or poor situations for a long period of time, you probably believe it to be you. It becomes your identity, your reality. So, it means acting as if you have it right now – acting as if you have total financial freedom, thinking and feeling that you've got an abundance of money, thinking and feeling that you're attracting that relationship into your reality, that you have that relationship and it's just about to come to you.

It means acting as if you have the outcome already – it's that simple.

Remember, if you're holding it in your mind and you're thinking and feeling all the positive things, your mind can't tell the difference between what you're imagining and what is true. So if it believes it's true – if you believe and think you're good enough, for example – your body will react to that. If you believe and think and feel abundant, you'll begin to attract that abundance into your life.

Focusing on your outcome is the key, and feeling good because it means you're giving that vibration of allowing, having the feelings of expectation, joy, abundance, happiness and prosperity to your body, and then your unconscious mind will match that signal to the thing that you need and want.

If you guide your emotions to the things you do want, they'll begin to manifest into your reality. What you think about, you'll bring about. And especially if you're thinking about them predominantly, if you've got them at the forefront of your mind – your unconscious and your conscious – you are going to begin to attract them into your reality. And don't worry about the negative thoughts at first; a positive thought outweighs a negative one because it has a higher frequency and a higher vibration.

Finding focus

Many people who set out on this journey may not see results as fast as they would like. They'll be thinking, acting and feeling positive, but then when it doesn't happen, or something bad happens, they'll just think this stuff doesn't work. But it's about consistency. When you have consistent positive feelings and thoughts of abundance, and consistent feelings of good health, you'll emit a positive frequency and attract the equal opposite and it will manifest into your reality. Think about the process as a journey to your destination. After all, you'd never set off on holiday and then just give up a third of the way there, would you? Of course not, you'd keep going because you have the direction, you have the map to get there.

Now you have the map, you need to find your focus.

Focus on what you want and feel gratitude for what you already have. If you maintain that focus, then you get to your destination. Then you become your potential.

Your thoughts no longer exist when you don't think of them; they're just not part of your reality anymore and become dormant. In the same way, when you don't think of the things that you want, they literally become nonexistent, because thoughts need attention. And the only way they don't get manifested, the only way those positive thoughts become dormant, is when we don't focus on *them* and focus on something else. Usually, it is focusing on the lack of something. If you think of something positive, only to then think of something negative, the positive thought becomes nonexistent; it has no life to it because you've literally cancelled it out.

All the people who have achieved great things and have succeeded in getting their outcomes – whether they are entrepreneurs or scientists, whether they are people who have the most amazing health or the most profound, loving relationships, or even great leaders, such as Martin Luther King – have one thing in common: they focused on their outcomes. They allowed them to become *dominant* in their minds. They put so much energy into getting their outcomes, only focusing on what they wanted to achieve.

Attracting your perfect health, wealth or happiness is not going to happen with a single thought, as it will simply lose its 'spark' or be replaced by another thought. However, when your thoughts become positive, focused and consistent, they begin to attract that specific outcome.

So if you have one positive thought, it will become a small vibration, a small frequency. However, the more times you have that positive thought, the more times you feel abundance, the more it will lead you to focus on your outcome. You begin to give it life; you begin to allow that vibration to amass itself to a level that will automatically begin to attract it into your life. The collective amount of positive feelings and thoughts will begin to yield much more than just one thought – your goals manifest. The more times you have that positive feeling, the more you begin to live and breathe that outcome as if you've got it right now in your life; the more that vibration begins to grow and give life to the vibrations of attracting that thing into manifestation.

Kevin's story

One of my clients had big money issues, in fact, big debt issues. He couldn't see a way out, and even considered suicide: he was in a very dark place. The more he focused on the debt, the more his life spiralled into overwhelming despair. Each negative thought gave life to more negative thoughts. I didn't have the power to change Kevin's financial situation, but I was able to give him a new, healthy way of thinking to drive and motivate him to be financially stable and attract the abundance he wanted.

First Kevin started to focus on having a positive outcome, and then we came up with an 18-month plan to get him back on track. We developed five actions he could do every week to start paying off his debts – little actions, but over time, they would build up momentum. The key was to change his focus from scarcity and despair to positive, focused drive. We made it a ritual that, just before he went to sleep each night, he would learn from what he'd done that day, so he could take those teachings into the next day to improve. Also, every morning he rehearsed in his mind how his day would go, putting his whole focus onto having a positive outcome – paying off the debt and attracting abundance. By combining what he had learned from the previous day and rehearsing his new day, Kevin's brain began to nourish and bathe his mind in healthy focused habits.

After one month, Kevin was still in debt, but he saw possibility in his future and had developed a newfound self-assurance and belief about getting back on track. After seven months he was way ahead of schedule with his repayments and felt unstoppable in his happiness. After 13 months he was free of debt and had savings; he also felt more content than ever before and had inner peace. The source of his happiness wasn't just his financial situation. He had discovered that he had choice and control over how he thought and felt, and that gave him real freedom.

With enough attention and intention to your desired outcome, the stronger it becomes, the stronger the desire at an unconscious level to find it. This, after time, will formulate new unconscious beliefs, new values, new attitudes and profound new resources and feelings within you. It will also begin to grow in all other areas of your life too. You'll begin to think, 'If I can achieve this here, I can also achieve this in another area', or 'If I'm good enough for that, then I'm easily going to be good enough to get that' or 'Now I've got successful relationships, I know I'm going to be able to attract the most wonderful, intimate relationship.' It's just generative learning.

Now I want you to carry on writing your gratitude list every morning when you wake up. Write down ten things that you really have gratitude for, so that you begin to have appreciation in your life.

I also want you to pick one of the five hypnosis audio download tracks from www.josephclough. com/byp – *The Perfect Health*, *Amazing Relationships*, *Financial Abundance*, *General Manifestation* or *Positive Affirmations*. Choose the one you really want to focus on.

When you listen to the hypnosis track – and it doesn't matter when you listen to it, as long as you listen to it and put your attention and intention into it – the suggestions will begin to imprint your unconscious mind with new beliefs, new feelings, new ways of acting and reacting to become aligned with getting your outcome. In alignment with manifesting and attracting anything that you want into your life – so you can have congruency – you can have pure wholeness within you, where you can truly feel contented with where you're going and what you're about to achieve into your life.

In the next chapter we will explore the power of thoughts further, and you'll learn more techniques for manifesting and being your potential.

Recap

- When negative thoughts come to your mind, it's your signal to focus on what you have – be grateful and take an attitude of appreciation – and use the opposites of the negative thoughts.

- Break free of past- and future-based thinking by living in the 'now'.

- Every thought is energy at a certain frequency that attracts its equal in reality. If you have feelings of gratitude, love, and self-worth, your mind will attract more of it into your life.

- Tune in to your thoughts and feelings and allow them to be in tune with your desires.

- Your mind can't tell the difference between real and imaginary, so go to the place you want to be in your mind and you will go there in reality.

- Your mind is a reflection of your outer world. You can allow yourself to be a product of what life is, or allow life to be a product of what you are – you choose.

Be Your Potential.

CHAPTER THREE

STEPPING UP

In the last chapter we discussed the importance of paying attention to our feelings and our emotions. Because when we focus on and think about all the things we don't want in our lives, we begin to attract them into our lives. Whatever you're thinking about, you're going to attract it. If you feel anger, you'll attract and feel more anger. If you feel fearful about situations, you're going to attract those fearful situations. However, if you focus on feeling good, feeling prosperous, abundant and joyful, you're going to start to attract those things into your life – you will start to be your potential.

If you're focusing on your problems, your mind will just continue to focus on the 'lack of'. You need to be able to retrain the mind, *consciously* and *unconsciously*, by thinking and feeling the positive things that you want to attract in your life – as if you have them right now. It's about shifting your focus onto what you want and how you want it.

Feeling good and thinking positively is simple when you use the hypnosis audio download tracks (www.josephclough.com/byp), as these techniques will help change your frame of mind from negative to positive and begin to allow positivity to manifest.

Let's take health as an example. If you focus on how poor your body is, or how bad your health is at present, you're going to get more of it – you'll be stuck in poor health. You would never drive a car by looking in the rearview mirror, would you? You look at where you are going. You put your focus ahead, outside the front windscreen, occasionally looking back – but mostly looking forward to your destination.

Moreover, I have found there can be a common trait in people with dis-ease or dis-order – they tend to focus on how their lives are at a disadvantage and send that signal throughout their whole bodies to act out that outcome. This way of thinking is called a *nocebo*, which means taking on a belief that causes harm, the opposite effect of a placebo.

But if we reconnect with our minds and bodies, we can focus our bodies to get well again, feeling good and being the way we want to be – healthy.

Overcoming stress

You have to notice where the stress is coming from, and choose to cut it out of your life, and then focus on the things that make you feel good.

So how do we notice where the stress is coming from?

The problem is that we rarely think about how others or things are creating stress within us. More often than not, we let stress into our mental environment without thinking about whether it is needed or good for us. Stress is a signal telling us to pay attention to a conflict – either within us or in our environment. A certain amount of stress is good for you, but free-ranging or long-term stress can have a negative effect on your state of mind, health and wellbeing.

What is the source of your stress? Consider what or who in your life is contributing to your inner stress and make a list of those things. By being conscious of stress, you can choose whether to allow it to hurt you, cut it out or modify how you react to it. Think about the stresses in your life and write down your responses to the following questions:

How would my life be different if the source of stress was out of my life?

Is that person or thing worth being unwell emotionally or physically?

Is there another way I can act or react that will allow that thing or person in my life?

If it's a person, are they aware of what they are doing, and are they willing to change too? If they are not, then am I prepared to allow them to dictate and affect my health?

What actions can I take now to remove the causes of stress?

You'll see that all the above questions come from a place that causes us to realize that *we allow* stress into our lives – no one else can create it for us unless we choose to accept it. Your health is far more important than allowing someone's actions to hurt you.

Remember, the more you think and act in a certain way, the more of the same you manifest. The more you think and feel good about life, the more those thoughts and feelings will begin to grow as well. Are you focusing on the good things, or on the things that are actually stopping you from getting what you want?

Although your positive thoughts and feelings may be few at first, the more you think and feel about what you desire, the easier you'll find it – positivity grows with momentum. As the thoughts become ingrained into your unconscious mind, and the more that they become ingrained into your unconscious, they will cement new beliefs, feelings, values and attitudes about life, and that's when your new focus begins to make changes in your life.

And now it's time to find the three missing keys that many people have forgotten in their lives, but which have always been there because we are, after all, pure potential.

It's now time for you to reconnect to your potential. By focusing on the things that you want to achieve, the whole process becomes very simple. In fact, the process of achieving the life that you want and becoming your potential can be broken down into three steps. It's simpler than you could ever imagine.

The first step is to **ask.**
The second is to **believe.**
The third is to **receive.**

Ask

Asking means to know your outcome – to know what you want and to be precise about it. To think as if you had it right now – and what it would be. What would be your desired outcome? Ask yourself these types of questions. Asking is the very start of the process of achieving your goals. Asking develops a clear intention and momentum within you. It is also a declaration of your self-worth: 'I want this because I am worthy of this'. If we do not ask we do not get.

Asking is the first step in instigating change.

I don't want you to think of goals that are small or average, I want you to make them bigger and better – goals that will completely change your life. I want you to think of exactly what you want in exactly the way you want it to happen – so embellish your 'wants' with as much detail as possible. Think how the goal or the outcome will also have an effect on you and everyone else around you, in the most wonderful and powerful way.

And don't set this goal to 'just getting by' or 'just having a good life'. You've got to set this goal towards 'pure excellence'. This is because, if you focus on an outcome to 'just get by', you may hit that goal or you may get just beneath it. By focusing on just getting 70 per cent, you may get just that, or a little bit less. However, if you focus beyond your expectations, if you focus on *pure excellence,* let's say 120 per cent, you may not hit the 120 per cent straight away, but you will hit 100 per cent.

So, you need to turn up the dial of your expectations, your dreams and your goals. To focus on absolute excellence and to get what you want out of life, which means setting your mind and your outcomes to more than you could ever imagine.

Remember, no matter what you think right now, you're more than that. Therefore you should intend more out of yourself, intend to achieve nothing less than your dreams, and then you can focus on them with clarity.

So the first step is asking: *What exactly do I want? How do I want it to happen?*

When you think about this, and think about your outcome, you're simply creating an idea – you're creating new thoughts. And as you create those thoughts, they become the vibrations, and as you create those vibrations, you're going to begin to attract the things that you want.

And the more you think about that idea, that outcome, the more you're going to really pull that into your reality. So focus on what you want and ask yourself: 'What do I want?' And forget about the excuses. Don't live up to those excuses, because if you think about them you're just going to expect them and get them.

Some people may think that they don't know what they want, but I truly believe that they do. I truly believe that everyone, really deep down inside, knows what they want but, because of their fears, doubts and excuses, they are prevented from thinking about what they want.

Don't buy into other people's excuses.

Other people's mindsets can stop us as well – I know, I've been there! So you've got to think to yourself now, are you buying into other people's thoughts? Other people's excuses? You just have to look at the media to see there's doubt, there's fear and there's worry everywhere, and you've got to ask yourself:

Do I want to buy into that fear?

Do I want to allow that fear and worry to be a part of my life?

Personally, I don't believe you should. I don't mean that you shouldn't listen to the news or read the newspapers, but you don't always have to take them seriously because it's not always true and you should refuse to allow it to have an effect on your life. Because if you refuse to allow it to have an effect on your life, you then have the strength to make changes in your world.

And what about our families? What excuses are we buying into there? If our parents said, 'You can't achieve that', or our siblings say, 'You can't do that, you'll never do it', are you buying into their excuses? Are you buying into other people's mindsets? Would you ever want your children to buy into the fear and doubt that you're buying into?

What about our partners, our friends, our colleagues? They all have a point of view, don't they? With the best of intentions I'm sure. However, you've got to ask yourself, if you take on their thoughts and their excuses as to *why* you shouldn't have something, surely you're just buying into their expectations, buying into that outcome for not getting what you want, and allowing fear and worry to creep into your life?

I personally think we should refuse to allow other people's mindsets to have an effect on what we think. You're in charge of your mind. Some people might say, 'How can I do that? How can I actually stop people's mindsets and the people around me having an effect on my life?' It doesn't mean it's going to be easy. However, you can decide to refuse to take their opinions, doubts and fears on board. As Viktor Frankl says in *Man's Search for Meaning,* 'When we are no longer able to change a situation, we are challenged to change ourselves'. Viktor chose to be in control and look toward the future, by having trust, hope and faith.

And there are many successful people who were told as children that they'd never amount to anything. Some people were told they would never be able to read or write, or hold down a job, and those people turned it around and actually utilized other people's doubts and used them as a motivation to succeed. They refused to take on other people's excuses, other people's expectations, because they were in charge of their minds and therefore their results.

Tom's story

Tom, one of my family members, was told that he had an aneurysm near his back and abdomen, and was given six months to two years to live. He was refused surgery because he was elderly and might not survive the operation, and told to live out his remaining life. Obviously, Tom felt distraught in every way possible, so I spoke to him about working with me to heal himself. Tom's doctor rubbished the idea, but fortunately Tom refused to listen and agreed to work with me. It took quite a few sessions, but we managed to clear out every negative emotion in his body. I put him on a healthy diet and made sure that he exercised. We worked hard to generate new beliefs, to tap into perfect health and to connect him to his potential. When he went back to his doctor again, his health was so much better that he was booked to have the operation as soon as possible, and when they measured the aneurysm it had actually decreased.

Tom's still alive – five years later – because he refused to take another person's reality on board; he believed that he could actually achieve anything he wanted – if he put his mind to it. Because of that he acted out his expectation of living, and having life, by focusing on the good things in life, like love, joy and happiness. He cleaned out his past so his body was actually free of negative emotions and he attracted good health in every way.

You can see how important it is not to buy into other people's excuses, other people's limitations. You're the only person who can buy into them; it's your choice. You have the power to refuse to allow those people or those things to have an effect on you right now. You can take responsibility – to be the real you.

Godlike powers

So when you think of the first process, of *asking*, thinking about what you want, think without limitations. Right now, in this moment, imagine.

Imagine having Godlike powers. Just imagine that everyone has a perception of what that may be like. Free of all limitations, being able to do anything, anyhow, in any way. Being free of fear, being free of worry or anxiety, and just imagine having all that potentiality to do anything you want.

- What would you do?

- What would you achieve today if you had those powers?

- How would you change your life?

- How would you change others around you in the most wonderful way?

- What difference would that make to you and everyone else?

It changes your thought processes, doesn't it? It makes you see reality without any limitations. I want you to begin to think that way. To think without limitations, because those limitations are just manmade – they're made by you. If you start creating and thinking the way that you want to, however, you can achieve and attract anything in your life and be your potential. And when you think about your outcome, make sure it is good for yourself and others.

You've got to have balance – making sure your desires are in harmony with others – because if you want bad things for others you're lowering your vibration once again. There will be incongruence within you. Make sure what you want is good for yourself and for others. Think about how it will have a benefit for everything else you do and for everyone else around you.

Everything I do has the conscious intention of being good for me and good for others – that's my aim. Yes, I generate money and have good wealth, but I'm doing it with the intention of helping others too. To allow people to have their lives the way they deserve to have them, free of limitations, and I'm very congruent within that.

So, when you think about your outcome – when you ask yourself, 'What do I want?' – make sure that it's good for you, it's good for your environment, it's good for the people around you. Because when you have that, you get pure congruency within you, you feel truly aligned in getting that outcome, and if it's good for you and good for others, you'll start to manifest it into your reality. And part of the asking process is to intend more out of yourself, to achieve your dreams in every way. But I want you to make those dreams bigger so they become your reality. And allow yourself to have the power of focus on them – focus with crystal clarity on your outcome.

And don't worry if you get doubts in your mind. Respond to the doubting thoughts by saying 'Thank you' to yourself, because the only reason you're having doubts is because you're not quite happy with the situation. In other words, you haven't got the result yet.

So, every time you get a negative or doubting thought, thank it and allow it to go. Release that thought and focus your thoughts back on your outcome again. So you can refocus your mind, and this will begin to send out the signal of vibration, an alignment to the outcome you want, and attract it into your reality. And if people doubt you, and you are buying into their excuses, then you've got to make a decision.

Are you going to choose to allow people to bring you down?

Are you going to choose to allow them to bring down your vibrations and energy?

Because you know what it's like, if you're around negative people you become negative. If you're around positive people you get positive. So you've got to think, where are you putting yourself, what environments are you putting yourself in?

You'll notice that the people who have finance problems tend to hang around with other people with money problems. And those people with relationship issues usually hang around with other people with relationship issues. People with poor health are usually around others who have poor health. Entrepreneurs, on the other hand, surround themselves with people who bounce ideas off each other, because it allows them to grow with more ideas, to be motivated by others with the same outcome or point of focus in mind.

So where are you choosing to *be* right now?

Who are you choosing to surround yourself with?

And if it's not the right people, search for new people who have the same intentions, the same goals and the same purposes as you. Surround yourself with people who are like-minded to your outcome – to what you want. I understand that you are where you are right now because it's familiar – it's all you know. It might seem easier to stay for many unconscious reasons – for example, habit, comfort and security – but you now have to make sure you put yourself around the right people. You have to step out of your situation and go beyond your present level to surround yourself with people who allow you to grow in every way.

So the first step is to *ask*, to know your outcome and have it in your mind all the time, and even more importantly, to feel it. Feel the feelings of having it already; allow your emotions to guide your thoughts, allow them to grow and, as they grow, your thoughts will begin to grow, your perceptions will begin to re-evaluate, to see what you really want to see and your mind will look out for those situations. Then it will begin to change your reality, to manifest outcomes to where you want to be in life.

Allow your feelings and your emotions to guide you towards your outcome.

Believe

The second step is to *believe*, and by believe I mean *anticipate*. To have an expectation of achieving your outcome, without any doubt, without any worries –

to truly know that it is going to happen and truly believe in it.

Because whatever you believe, you will begin to manifest. Our beliefs are the most powerful things that we have, because if we believe in something very strongly we're going to manifest it to be true. Studies have shown that there is one main thing that allows people to get healthy when they are ill – no matter what treatment they've used, whether it is hypnosis, chemotherapy, radiotherapy, reiki, spiritual healing, you name it – and that is their *belief* that they're going to get better. Even if they didn't use any form of therapy but just had the belief that they were going to get through it. That is a powerful criteria, because they have the belief that they 'want to get better' and they believe they will get better.

Bruno Klopfer

There is a wonderful story in *The Holographic Universe* by Michael Talbot, which turned my perceptions inside out. It's about the psychologist Bruno Klopfer, who was treating a man named Wright with advanced cancer of the lymph nodes. All standard treatments had been exhausted, and Wright appeared to have little time left. But he had heard about an exciting new drug and begged his doctor to let him try it. At first his doctor refused because the drug was only being tried on people with a life expectancy of at least three months, but Wright just wouldn't give in. So eventually the doctor gave Wright an injection of this drug, but in his heart of hearts he didn't expect Wright to last the weekend. The following Monday he found Wright out of bed and walking around, and Klopfer reported that his tumours were half their original size. Ten days after Wright's first treatment, he left the hospital and was, as far as the doctors could tell, in remission.

He remained well for about two months, but then articles began to appear reporting that this drug actually had no effect on the cancer or the lymph nodes. Wright, who was rigidly logical and scientific in his thinking, became very depressed, suffered a relapse and was readmitted to hospital. This time however, the physician decided to try an experiment. He told Wright this drug was every bit as effective as it had seemed, but some sort of initial supplies of the drug had deteriorated during shipping. He explained that he had a new, highly concentrated version of the drug and could treat Wright with this. Of course, the physician didn't really have a new version of the drug and injected Wright with a placebo. Again, the results were dramatic – the tumour masses melted, the chest fluid vanished and Wright was quickly back on his feet again, feeling great.

He remained symptom-free for another two months, but then the American Medical Association announced that a nationwide study of this drug had found it worthless in the treatment of cancer. This time, Wright's faith completely altered. His cancer blossomed and he died two days later.

Although Wright's story is tragic, it contains a powerful message. When we are able to bypass our limiting beliefs and tap into the healing forces within us, we can potentially cause tumours to melt away overnight. It makes you wonder, doesn't it? About your belief and what it can do for you? And equally important, what your belief can do against you.

What beliefs are stopping you from achieving your outcome of having that perfect relationship? Or knowing that you could have all the financial abundance that you deserve and that you could have the perfect health if you truly desire it? It's just a matter of your beliefs, and you can choose to transcend your limiting beliefs and instead have ones that will support you and allow you to be in alignment in getting your goals and outcomes.

So, we've talked about the first and second steps, asking and knowing your outcome and how important belief is too, in actually believing, trusting, anticipating and expecting your outcome to happen.

And within that, also keeping your positive emotions up, allowing them to be focused on your outcome, feeling good and having gratitude for where you are right now.

Don't let your beliefs hold you back

Receive

And the third and final step in getting what you want is to simply *receive*. This is the art of inspired action, which means following your intuition and taking action – choosing your line, as Viktor Frankl did when he arrived at Auschwitz. But it doesn't mean doing things you don't want to do. I don't believe you will achieve your outcomes by doing the things you are simply loath to do.

So, if you feel that you have to work hard, or do a form of action you don't like, I would say just simply don't do it. When the moment happens you'll know that you want to do it; when you feel there's an opportunity to get your outcome and it feels right with you. So your actions must be aligned with your true values, wants and needs in getting your outcome. When you feel inspired to make that decision, and your intuition – your inner voice – tells you that it is right to follow through with action, that's when you achieve your dreams. We'll cover this in more detail in the 'five steps to success' in Chapter 5.

This third step of receiving is about putting your mind to where you want it to go. Focusing your mind in the right direction of your goal, and allowing those events to unfold in achieving your outcome. Remember that your thoughts are vibrations, and those vibrations are emitting into your reality.

Imagine each of your thoughts as a droplet of water – the thoughts might be related to your health, your relationships, career or finances. When the droplet falls into water – reality – it creates ripples. Your thoughts go out into your reality and ripple outward throughout life. So your thoughts simply ripple out into your reality. The more 'thought droplets' you have, the bigger the ripples in your reality. So one thought can lead to a mass of thoughts, which creates and sends signals to attract the same back to you. In this way, you become aligned to your outcome.

So your thoughts, vibrations and energy must match your desired outcome. And that is the art of simply receiving – having gratitude, expectation and enjoying the journey to your life-changing results. And remember, it's not about controlling your thoughts, either. It's about guiding them, and the best way to guide them is by allowing yourself to have your emotions aligned in getting your outcome. Those positive feelings of love, gratitude, happiness and inner fulfillment then become your values, your guidance, and your focus.

It's also very important to live in the 'now', and you can do this by putting your attention onto what is happening in the present. More often than not, we get caught up in our past and our future and we miss out on all the wonderful things happening right now. All change and transformation happens in the now, peace and contentment are only to be found in the now and to really live is to put our attention in the now, this moment in time. Now I know that in real life 'stuff' happens – we live in a fast-paced world – so how do we do this in reality?

Well, I have the perfect way to pull you back to the present moment. We get caught up in the past because our minds are trying to look back to see if they can help us, and we think about the future because we want to plan for what might happen, so you could say there's a positive reason for why we get caught up in past- and future-based thinking and forget about the beauty of now. So here are the steps:

Step 1

When you wake up, spend about ten minutes rehearsing your day, setting out your intentions as to how you want it to go and how you want to be positive. This takes care of your obsessing over the future negatively, or becoming anxious in general.

Step 2

As you go to sleep each night take about ten minutes to review your day and preserve positive teachings that will help you the next day. Ask yourself 'What can I learn from today that, once learned, will allow me to grow as a person and be safer and happier?' This takes care of dwelling on negative events in the past, as you can leave your past where it belongs and simply take the lessons learned with you.

Step 3

Finally, throughout the day, take five minutes in each hour to sit peacefully, take in your environment and be aware of your thoughts. Then allow your thoughts to be aware of what's happening in your experience and what you can notice. Enjoy just *being* for a while. This allows you to live in the now, and the more you do this, the more the present will expand into more of your day and lead you to be happier and more productive.

The above process allows you to still live in the real world, while being safe and prepared, but also to really experience living in the moment in peace.

Because I can promise you that material things won't make you truly happy. They will of course have an effect on your mindset and emotional wellbeing, but it is not the real happiness. You make yourself happy. When you have inner contentment – inner wholeness – then you appreciate those external things even more. People always strive for external things, don't they? I'm sure you do. I know I do, and I'm not saying it's a bad thing, but we've also got to pay attention to what's happening in us now and enjoy the present. A lot of the time people work to get a bigger and better house, and once they've got that, they want a bigger one. Once they've got their new car they're looking up to the next model. Once we've got the material, we outgrow it and want something more than that – we raise the bar. But sometimes people get into that state of *only* wanting more and more and more, without appreciating the now and having meaning in the now, because the present has meaning if you choose.

You can choose to have gratitude and contentment in your life. Those external things will not make you happy if you're not truly content in yourself. So it's very important to embrace the present moment and put yourself in a good state of mind, because once again, that raises your vibrations towards the thing that you actually want to achieve as well. Allowing that wholeness to grow from within, and then externally appreciating those things in the most wonderful way, rather than the other way round.

You can choose to feel good right now.

Create your feeling

So what I'd like you to do now is to be able to create a feeling that you can have, apply and trigger whenever you wish. This process will allow you to change your emotional state at will:

- From feeling anxious to instantly feeling calm and assured.

- From procrastinating to being motivated and driven.

- From being unconfident to being completely confident and secure within yourself.

- From feeling fearful to transforming yourself to a feeling of safety.

The possibilities are endless – whatever your negative emotional state, you can change it in an instant, and furthermore train your mind to do this naturally with a little practice.

It's about teaching your body to change your internal state at will. You can create a powerful association to your body, so that every time you apply a certain stimulus (called an anchor in NLP) to your body while feeling an emotion, the two become neurologically interlinked. For example, if you were to get in a state of true happiness and then you applied a certain stimulus, i.e. a firm touch on a part of your body, the two would become hardwired together – the feeling and the stimulus. So every time you apply the stimulus, you unleash the feeling.

Anchoring is an application of an effect known as classical conditioning – the idea of creating a conditioned response to an external stimulus – that was first shown in a famous experiment by Russian psychologist Ivan Petrovich Pavlov. Pavlov conditioned a group of dogs to salivate when they heard a bell ring. He caused this response by ringing a bell and giving the dogs food at the same time. He continued ringing the bell and offering the dogs food until, after a period of time, the dogs salivated when they heard the bell and no food was offered – the sound and the response were hardwired together.

I used this technique on myself to see if it worked, long before I became a therapist, with amazing results. I had a job interview and, as always, I knew this high-pressure situation would cause me to blush, get anxious and freeze. When I fired off my own 'anchor' as I walked into the interview, something very strange happened. It was a transformation. I felt so calm, so cool and confident, no matter what question was asked. I breezed through the interview and got the job. I was so amazed at how easy it is to change your emotional state.

Now wouldn't it be of value to be able to do the exact same thing by using the other modality of just touch? So every time you applied a certain stimulus your body would have the cue to be able to feel a certain way. Imagine being able to feel powerful. To feel gratitude, motivation or happiness. The options are endless, but it's all about controlling your emotional state.

So, no matter what you're feeling, if you apply that stimulus to your body you'll automatically begin to feel the way that you want to, therefore becoming aligned with your feelings – aligned with your outcome.

Creating an anchor

I have recorded an audio version of this powerful process, called *Change Your Emotional State Process,* which you can download at www.josephclough.com/byp, so I can guide you personally. In the meantime, if you want to try it for yourself, read through the following and then close your eyes and relive the process in your mind.

Start by having a feeling that you would truly like to have whenever you wanted – it could be absolute gratitude, happiness, drive or motivation. No matter what it is, I want you to think about that one thing and close your eyes; I want you to see yourself being that way, with the emotion fully present. Maybe you've had the powerful emotion in the past, so make that memory really vivid. Go ahead right now and see yourself having that emotion – or see yourself acting as if you've had that emotion. Now put it on a movie screen in front of you. As you see yourself in your mind's eye, just turn up the picture, to make it bigger and brighter, and make it clearer and clearer. Intensify the colour of the movie so that it's realistic and seems real.

Now step inside the picture, really see what you would be seeing. See the kaleidoscope of beauty of you experiencing that powerful emotion in the present moment. Turn up the picture even more, as if there's a dial in front of you, just turn up that picture. See yourself and hear the thoughts of what you would be saying, and enjoy the empowering feeling – your feeling – of how wonderful it is to feel like this right now. Turn up the tonality in your mind (even overload the image) and make it even more encouraging; really hear what you'd be hearing having that feeling right now.

And then turn up that feeling and increase it, allow that feeling to spin faster and faster inside your body, and as it spins faster and faster, turn up that feeling even stronger, and as you turn up that feeling allow the picture to get bigger and better, brighter and stronger. Intensify the sounds – the feeling spinning all the way around – until you're feeling so good you can't stop it. And then, when you're feeling the emotion at its peak level, squeeze your thumb and finger together, feeling that feeling and having it right now – stronger and stronger – and allow that feeling to grow stronger as you push your fingers together. And as that feeling grows, really squeeze your fingers together and really keep that feeling right there.

So every time you squeeze those fingers together, you'll be able to access this feeling whenever you deserve it or whenever you wish. And then just open your eyes again.

Now go ahead and close them again. As you release your fingers, see yourself in that movie again, acting, feeling and reacting the way that you want.

Now what I'd like you to do is to keep repeating the same process – get in touch with the feeling, really turn up the feeling and squeeze the thumb and finger together once the feeling is at its peak. Repeat this process until that 'good' feeling is really stacked – feeling upon feeling.

To test whether you have set this positive anchor, I'd like you to squeeze your thumb and finger together the exact same way and notice what happens. You should notice that the same feeling builds up inside of you. If it's not as strong as you'd like it, I want you to repeat the process until the emotion is really stored and associated neurologically on your finger and thumb each time they are squeezed together. Because the more times you repeat the process, the more it becomes engrained inside of you. We're training your unconscious mind to change your state whenever you want.

I would also suggest that, whenever you feel this positive feeling naturally in day-to-day situations, you squeeze those fingers together again. In this way, you stack up that 'good-feeling' association. This allows you to compound the powerful feeling with these new feelings, so every time you wake up in the morning you can fire off that trigger and really feel good in every way.

And that's a simple way of changing your state and being aligned with your outcome, and you can do it for anything. You can have more than one emotion stacked up on the thumb and finger, you can stack it up with plenty of feelings so whenever you squeeze the thumb and finger together, you can change your state of mind.

It's the exact same stimulus response to when you turn on the radio and you hear the wonderful song that you really love. It just changes your mindset, it changes your physiology – it makes you feel good. This is what we're doing right now, but you can artificially create that in your neurology. You can retrain your mind to think and feel the way that you want to.

Allow yourself to feel good

By now your vibrations, your thoughts and your feelings should be aligned with getting your outcome. Refusing to allow what other people are saying to you will have a positive effect. Now you know that you don't have to buy into their excuses or their limitations. However, you can choose to listen to yourself, because when the external noise – the external things going around you – clouds your intuition you know that something is not right. But if you allow your feelings, your thoughts and your intuition to outgrow the sounds around you, then you know you're heading in the right direction and are ready to simply receive. So trust your intuition to have that inspired action of doing what feels right for you, and simply allow events to unfold in achieving what you want – to be your potential.

Allow your thoughts to make you feel good, as they begin to be your own new values. Values for living with abundance, values for living with happiness, contentment, congruency and free of conflict in every way. So remember, if you have a negative thought, flip it around and find its polar opposite – because that negative thought is just telling you that something's not right. Respond by appreciating that thought for that second, and then allowing it to release itself before focusing on exactly where you want to be and living abundantly – in your health, your relationships and your career.

Go ahead and continue to listen to your chosen hypnosis audio track (*Perfect Health, Amazing Relationships, Financial Abundance, General Manifestation* or *Positive Affirmations* at josephclough. com/byp), and remember to write down the ten things that you feel gratitude for, every day.

Put yourself in a feeling of gratitude – living, feeling the abundance inside of you and truly continuing the process of unlocking your true potential in every way.

Recap

- The process of getting what you want starts with knowing your outcome.

- Use the three steps – ask, believe and receive – in a way that sets out a declaration for achieving your goals, while developing the self-belief and feelings to succeed in all areas of your life.

- Know that the mind can't distinguish between what is imagined and what is true, and utilize your mind in a way that causes you to visualize your own success and be your potential.

- Understand the importance of acknowledging your intuition and allowing it to guide your thoughts and inspired action.

- Change your emotional state at will by setting up and using anchors.

- Remember, the more good feelings that you experience, the more those feelings and thoughts begin to simply grow in every way. And as those feelings and thoughts and energy grow, you begin to attract the same back to you.

Be Your Potential.

CHAPTER FOUR

TIME TO LET GO

In this chapter you will be setting off on your journey to get your results. Think about this process as a voyage to rid yourself of past limitations. Because, if you think about it, if your mindset – the way that you act and react – is dependent on your thoughts and feelings, you need to make sure you have clean, clear feelings that are aligned with getting your outcome. Therefore you need to be able to raise your thoughts to a level that will get your outcome – so you have the most excellent relationships, you transform your finances beyond a level that you've ever dreamed of and reconnect with perfect health in every way.

I'm sure you've noticed that you sometimes have limiting thoughts or beliefs about yourself. You may be thinking, 'I really want to be able to have the most amazing relationship, but all men or all women are bad; they always hurt me'. Or you may feel 'not good enough' to have that relationship or that you're 'not worthy' of having financial abundance in your life. The limiting decisions or beliefs that you may have towards your dreams have to go – now. This includes beliefs such as 'it's hard to have financial success', or the reasons and decisions that you have made to feel dis-ease in your body, to feel unwell and have medical issues. It's very important that in order to get where we want to be, we need to clean out those limiting decisions.

And we need to let go of the negative emotions that can bring us down too – the unhappiness, the anger, the sadness, the fear, the guilt, the hurt and the frustration, you name it. We need to get rid of those so we can 'clear' ourselves. And by 'clear' I mean to resolve and dissolve every little bit of conflict within so you get 100 per cent alignment in getting your outcome. So you just know you're going to achieve your results, achieve your dreams and outcomes in the most wonderful way without any conflict or block.

When you feel congruent in yourself, your potential will start to flow and your outcomes will happen.

Getting clear

This is exactly where we're heading now. And we're going to be covering two processes which allow that to happen. The first process is about cleaning the now, and making sure that you're in the right state of mind – free of those negative emotions and issues. And then later on we're going to be talking about how we can clean all our negative past experiences so they no longer affect us in the present.

Because the way I see it, if we've had 'X' number of negative experiences – of not getting our outcome, not having wonderful relationships, not having our health the way we want it, or poor associations with money – they begin to get compounded in our unconscious and affect our present ability to achieve our potential. Therefore, every time we go into a new situation, we have those emotions and limiting thoughts in the present situation. Because every action we're making right now is being guided by our past memories or by 'inspired action'. We want to go by 'inspired action', when we just *know* what to do and how to do it, having released all those negative associations to past events. We become programmed to have negative associations and limiting decisions towards our goals due to past events that we have gone through. For example, if you have had bad relationships or a bad financial track record, or have been plagued by poor health over the years, you're more likely to develop negative associations towards those areas in your life. This causes you to act and react in a programmed way – rather than by using 'inspired action'.

We want to get rid of those old behaviours and install a wonderful new mindset – a life-enhancing system that allows you to manifest those dreams.

If you will, I would like you to paint this picture in your mind. Imagine a memory – it doesn't matter whether it is good or bad, as long as it's charged with an emotion. If you've gone through bad events, the memory is probably going to be charged with a negative emotion – anger, sadness, fear, guilt, hurt or unhappiness. However, good memories – perhaps a great birthday, or when you've had a joyous event in the family, or when you once achieved a personal goal – are charged with a positive emotion. So when you look back to a particular memory you're going to have a certain feeling attached to it.

Your unconscious mind remembers those memories with the emotion attached. It remembers those things that are significant to you. It forgets the memory of brushing your teeth in the morning ten years ago on a given date. But it keeps the events that had an *effect* on your body. And once again, that goes for the positive and the negative events.

And the primary reason why your unconscious holds that negative emotion is simply for your own protection. If you go through a negative situation your unconscious mind does not want you to go there again. So it stores that negative emotion so that every time you go into a similar future situation, it will produce those feelings and mindsets. So the intention is good but the behaviour isn't going to get you the results.

You don't need that unwarranted fear or anger or sadness every time you venture into a new situation. But there are simple ways in which you can let go of them and still be protected. Ways where you clean out the negative emotion and replace it with positive learning. If you can get your unconscious mind to learn from situations, it won't need to keep that negative emotion anymore because it knows what to do and how to react – it will be safe. And that's a simple process that we will be venturing on to later in the chapter.

Three simple words

First, I'd like you to start the process of cleaning out the 'now'. This process comes from *Ho'oponopono*, which is an ancient Hawaiian practice or ritual of reconciliation and forgiveness. This process says that we can change our world, and the people in it, by changing ourselves. Okay, it sounds a little bit out there, for someone to be able to heal someone else, but there's a definite premise behind it that can transform and transcend your own thinking.

When you think about it, if we are all fundamentally interconnected then it is possible to change other people by our thoughts and actions. If our 'vibrations' – our 'energy' – and our thoughts are linked to the outside world then if we change our 'inside' world and clean and clear our minds of conflict, we can then go ahead and begin to perceive, project and manifest the 'outer' reality in which we really want to live.

But to be honest, you don't have to believe the theory, because this process works beyond that. It's all down to four sayings, and predominantly, three simple words: 'I love you'.

'I love you' – those are the most powerful three words we can ever say to another person, or even ourselves, aren't they? They are the purest of words; they can send a warm tingle down your spine if said by the one you love. As I said earlier, all other emotions are manmade but love is infinite. Love has no end and no beginning. It's about a pure 'beingness'. Now if you were to have love in every aspect of your life, it would truly transform and transcend the way you perceive your reality, wouldn't it? If you have complete love in your mind and body, I believe it will simply heal itself, because the frequency, the vibration, and the healing of the emotion of love, will simply resolve the conflict.

If you have love in your body you can't have the stresses and strains that break the chain of good health. I believe that love will fix that chain in every way. When it comes to things like relationships, if you begin to have an abundance of real love for yourself and also love for the person you're about to attract into your life, the frequency of those thoughts and feelings will begin to attract the alike and manifest what you desire.

And money. Think about it – if you have wonder, gratitude and love for the financial rewards you want to manifest, it's going to come to you cleaner and clearer because there's no negative associations to money if you just have love for it. And I mean love in a pure way, not a greedy way but just a pure way of being and living in this world.

Fundamentally, this process allows new associations to everything. To develop those associations so you get clean and clear about your goals.

And remember I said earlier that every action that you're taking right now is being guided by past memories or by inspired action? So if you are being run by memories in this present moment, then you need to clean and clear them. Now if you were to have love for all the situations you've been in, and treated them as teachings, and began having that love towards those situations or people, then you're going to begin to dilute those past negative emotions and therefore become cleaner and clearer within your mind.

If you are clean and clear of negative emotions in all situations, and your mind and body are aligned and saturated with positive feelings, you will change *all* the situations that you're in.

If nothing else, your association has changed to that situation. So if everything is a mental projection as such, you get what you want by thinking and feeling about it. And by doing this process you begin to radiate the feeling of love throughout your whole body. Now if you radiate that feeling, other people pick up on your intention. It goes into your environment, and if nothing else, you begin to have happier days because you're in a joyful, grateful and loving state of mind.

So let's test it out.

Step 1

Go ahead and think of an issue. It could be a health issue, or your current mindset – maybe you think that you're 'not good enough' to get the finances that you want, or you may be thinking that 'it's too hard'. Or possibly you may have a belief about yourself that isn't working for you at present. Maybe there's someone in your life who just annoys you, or you have negative associations to him or her.

Step 2

As you think about that someone or something, hold the image in your mind, and as you hold that image in your mind, just keep repeating the words 'I love you. I love you. I love you'. And the more you keep saying it right now, allow it to become your own internal self-talk – 'I love you. I love you' – and allow your internal self-talk to be bathed in love, give love and feel love. You will notice it begins to change the way that you think about that association in no time at all.

Step 3

Keep repeating the process as often as you can, because the more you do, the more you dissolve your negative emotional associations to the problem. This in turn causes you to have new insights, and it will set you free to see life clearly and in peace.

Transcending your perceptions

This simple but powerful process allows you to start to connect with new neuro-associations of gratitude and love towards those people and situations that were causing negative emotions within you. Before long, you'll begin to notice something quite strange. You'll be aware that your health issue will ease, that the other person will begin to change, that the limiting belief about yourself will be saturated with a new feeling of love and gratitude for who you really are.

Make this process part of your self-talk on a day-to-day basis. Imagine, if you have that loving feeling and those loving words inside your mind in all situations, they will begin to transcend how you perceive your health, other people and even yourself. And if you transcend your perceptions, you'll begin to transform your behaviour and 'how' you act and react.

As the intention of your behaviour and reactions changes it will raise the vibrations of your thoughts and feelings to match the intention or outcome that you're really going for. I'd like to think that we would all aim for a loving feeling – whether it's to be loved by someone, to love your job, to love your body, to love the people who are in your reality or to develop greater relationships. In starting this process, therefore, you begin to do this – you begin to saturate those old negative feelings in the now and begin to replace them with feelings of love and gratitude.

And when you think about it, where you are right now is having a 'lack of' in some way. You haven't got all your results. By replacing those old feelings with positive ones you're reaffirming to yourself, sending a signal to get your mind and body into alignment of where you want to be – to have enhanced happiness, wholeness, contentment and alignment in achieving your outcome. And we all strive for that in every way.

Forgive me, I'm sorry and thank you

Now there are three other sayings too. We have 'I love you', but also 'Forgive me', 'I'm sorry', and 'Thank you'.

But what does 'I'm sorry' really mean? What does it actually do to your body? Actually, it's very powerful because, when you say 'I'm sorry', it releases past negative emotions such as guilt.

You're releasing those negative emotions upon your body by simply saying 'I'm sorry'. When you hear someone say 'I'm sorry' it gives you a sense of freedom, a sense of knowing that something's happened. A release.

'Forgive me' couples with 'I'm sorry' because it enforces forgiveness and releases the past. You can't undo the past but you can refuse to allow past events and situations to have an effect on your life in the present. So you can say, 'I'm sorry', 'Forgive me' and then, 'Thank you'.

Thank you is a wonderful way of saying that something has been achieved and that it's done and over with. Your past issues are the past now – they are over with.

It's also powerful just to *know* you're going to achieve your outcome, having thanks just knowing you're going to achieve your goals, giving thanks that your mind and body are getting back into true alignment. So by saying 'Thank you', you're acting as if it's already achieved – that to me is true expectation.

So, on all levels of your mind and body, we're literally changing how you perceive the now, the present situations, and getting your results in a way that you want them.

So, everything I do right now, I say, 'I love you', because it begins to connect a new sense of feeling inside me – it just makes me feel good. A feeling of 'love' and 'contentment' for life gives me gratitude, even in situations where I'm not quite happy, when things aren't going my way. I've noticed that when I say the words 'I love you' it begins to change the way I perceive that event too. So if I'm stuck in traffic and I just think to myself, 'I love you', it begins to change the way I'm feeling in the present moment. It begins to focus my attention on the things I love and the things that are good in my life. When I'm working with my clients in a one-to-one consultation, I try to radiate a wonderful feeling of love in the most pure form. And I've noticed that every time I've used this process, my clients recover much quicker. And I really believe it's about my honest true feeling of love for everything and everyone in my life, because in some way I've attracted them into my reality. My clients come to see me for help, and so I take responsibility to resolve their issue. When I project love and gratitude towards them it begins to transform my physiology, my tonality and also my thinking towards that client. And they pick up on this feeling; they pick up on the real, pure honesty and the genuine feeling that I want to help them. So this process can vitally improve your relationships with everything and everyone in your reality.

The feeling of love can transcend and transform your environment and the way that you perceive all situations. And once again, that heightens your vibrations and emotions, it enlightens your thoughts and feelings, which will guide you to where you want to be.

If you're focusing on past negative emotions or present negative emotions of frustration, anger, sadness, fear, guilt, hurt or even unhappiness, those emotions stop you in your tracks from being your potential. They stop you and block you from achieving your outcome. But if you can really saturate those feelings with a sense of wellbeing, wholeness, gratitude and love in all areas of life, it changes everything that you're connected to, it changes the way your mind and body are communicating with each other.

The mind has a vital effect on the body – create wellbeing in your mind and your body will respond accordingly.

People who feel unhappy in their lives can begin to talk down to themselves; they might say things like, 'How stupid I am. I'm terrible – life's not worth living. I'm not good enough. I can't achieve that. Life's just bad'. This sends a signal throughout their whole neurology to feel negatively about themselves. Deep-seated feelings of unhappiness cause the body to feel sadness, doubt, nervous anxiety and to suffer from low energy levels. As a result, these strong emotions and reactions can cause a dis-order in the person's body because they feel conflicted. It lowers their energy. You rarely see an unhappy person with an abundance of energy. Or hear them saying, 'I'm so unhappy in life – but I can't stop jumping up and down because of all this energy!' – of course you don't!

People suffering with deep-seated feelings of unhappiness always have a lack of energy. They always have a lack of wanting to do something and they don't feel proactive. And those people who have had bad relationships are always thinking negatively towards other people and themselves.

Now if you think and focus on those negative results, you bring about those negative results and people. And those people who have poor associations to money – they feel they're not good enough to get it, or that you need to put in a lot of hard work just to get by in life, it demotivates them – they have a lack of energy. But by saturating those negative thoughts with feelings of love and real gratitude, you can change your associations to them. So you begin to perceive money as a loving thing, a natural process whereby you can actually get money and then utilize it to help others around you – whether that is by helping out a friend, or giving a percentage to charity or treating your children. You can allow your abundance to spread for the greater good.

Money *isn't* bad! People perceive it as bad or hard to get, but it doesn't have to be that way. Many entrepreneurs have all the money they want and they use it to fund wonderful charitable projects. Think about Sir Richard Branson for example: having made all his money he now devotes himself to putting quite a lot of it back into good causes (www.virginunite.com). In doing so, he's able to help other people to realize their dreams. Bill Gates (and Melinda Gates for that matter) is another great example of a successful entrepreneur who gives a phenomenal amount of money to charitable causes (www.gatesfoundation.org). They are just two examples of successful people with an abundance of money who use it for the greater good. But no matter what we earn, we should all strive to help people around us, so that when good things happen in our lives we can spread that along to others. I can tell you now, people feel better giving than receiving. And when we spread our wealth to other people it means that we actually get more from it, because our associations become feelings of gratitude – gratitude for ourselves, our environment and for the people around us.

When it comes to your health, if you have loving feelings and you send the signals to yourself of love and wellbeing, your body becomes in sync with those feelings too. This is why happy people tend to suffer less illness than those with a lot of stress or significant emotional events in their lives. The latter lack wellbeing, because their emotional conflicts cause their bodies to have a reaction of illness. Those people who are happy, abundant and loving in their lives send signals that everything is going well to each part of their neurology – they send that self-worth and self-love to themselves and therefore it begins to grow as well.

The same is true of relationships. Having love for yourself and love for the person who is in your life – or who you want to bring into your life – develops the right environment for a successful relationship and enhances your communication with yourself and others. If you have a relationship, it will become stronger and if you want a relationship you will attract the right relationship into your life.

So I want you to try doing this process over the next few days and allow it to become a vital part of your life.

Step 1

When you wake up in the morning, say the words 'I love you'. This sets you up for the day.

When I had low self-esteem, I started doing this. I would look in the mirror and spend a few minutes just saying 'I love you'. It felt awkward at first, even slightly wrong, but I wanted to interrupt my low self-esteem pattern, and after doing it for a month, I began to not only say it, but actually feel it too. That's not ego, that's natural self-expectance for how amazing you are – you are amazing!

Step 2

When bad things happen to you, just say, 'I love you'.

When we do this, it stops our negative reactions and it causes us to dissociate and also get deep insight and perspective on the situation. It also transcends our perception to one of love. Try this one out and notice what happens – you will be surprised!

Step 3

When good things happen to you, say, 'I love you'.

This reinforces your self-acceptance and self-worth for all the good things in your life. It's a form of gratitude that will allow more good things to flow your way.

Step 4

Throughout your day just repeat the mantra of 'I love you' whenever it feels right to you.

Want more love in your relationships? More love in your career? More love in your health? More love in your money? More love for life? Then you must give more love, and by repeating 'I love you' throughout the day that love will evolve in every aspect of your life!

Because once again if nothing else, it makes you feel good, and don't you want to feel good? Of course you do. The other three sentences are 'I'm sorry', 'Forgive me' and 'Thank you'.

Freeing yourself of past negative emotions

Now this next process we're moving onto is about deeper clearing of negative emotions; letting go of those inappropriate and unwarranted emotions or limiting decisions you may have that limit your potential.

So for example, you may have beliefs towards money that it's 'too hard to get'. You may have beliefs about yourself that you're 'not good enough' or 'not worthy'. Or you might be holding beliefs about your health, such as 'I can't heal myself', or 'I can't achieve the results that I want' or 'I can't have a good, healthy body'.

Now it's time to start thinking about the beliefs that limit you and you would love to let go of. The ones that stop you from doing and achieving what you want in your life. So go ahead and take a few minutes right now to write down some of the negative emotions that you want to get rid of. These might include feelings such as anger, guilt, hurt, sadness, fear, frustration and so on.

Even if you are experiencing a general feeling of conflict within yourself, go ahead and write that down too. And then even write down your limiting decisions. What are the obstacles and blocks getting in the way of you achieving your outcome? What are the limiting thoughts, the limiting mindsets that prevent you from being your potential? Just go ahead and write them down under the following headings:

- Limiting beliefs, for example, feeling 'not good enough'.

- Unwarranted emotions, for example, anger, sadness, guilt.

Look at your list and recall Chapter 1 where I talked about the prime directives of the unconscious mind.

We learned that:

- The unconscious does everything for a positive intention.

- Your body is always trying to protect you in some way.

- Your unconscious stores memories as emotions and preserves and maintains the integrity of the body.

But a few others would be:

- The unconscious mind represses memories with unresolved negative emotion. So if your body hasn't dealt with a significant emotional event, it will just keep the emotion attached to it for protection.

- It represses negative emotions or limiting decisions to protect you in the future.

For example, if you go through a negative event, a significant one where you have a lot of emotions – let's say you were hurt in a past relationship – you still carry that hurt and even fear that it may happen again. Every time you go into a new relationship, you remember the hurt and you fear that it will happen again. Although you may know that person is perfect in every way, you still hold onto the negative emotion because your unconscious mind is trying to protect you.

The unconscious mind will hold onto negative emotions such as fear – even extreme fears such as phobias – so every time you go into that situation the unconscious tries to protect you by saying 'Look, don't go near that, it's scary, it may hurt you'. Although logically we know that the thing isn't going to hurt us, our unconscious mind thinks that it will and it therefore holds on to that phobia or fear.

Wouldn't it be of so much value to be able to release those past negative emotions? Wouldn't it be so valuable to simply get clear in yourself, so you feel 100 per cent congruent going into a relationship, knowing that he or she isn't the person who hurt you in the past and that they could be the one? To keep the teachings from the past, so that you always remain protected, without the unwarranted fear or hurt.

Wouldn't it be of value to let go of the negative emotion that your body has been holding for so long? What would happen if you were to let go of all those repressed negative emotions? Wouldn't it just be a weight off your shoulders? Imagine feeling as if you simply let go of all that negativity, and just focus on the day's teachings and the positive outcomes you've enjoyed.

How would that feel?

What about the negative emotions towards money, or the limiting decisions that you've made to not actually attract it into your life? What would happen if you let go of those today and had an undeniable experience of it?

Wouldn't that simply be magical?

And once again, if you recall, I explained how your past memories are held at an unconscious level and those past memories, if they are significant to you, will be charged with a positive or a negative emotion. And once the conscious or unconscious mind preserves the teachings from those events, or just the past in general, then it won't need to hold that emotion any more. It can simply release it knowing that the body has a more efficient, more congruent way of keeping you safe and protected.

Because learning from teachings is a safer way of being. If you've learned from the past or learned from a situation, you just simply know what not to do. And you simply know *what* to do because you've learned from it. And it's much more efficient than having fear, anger, hurt, sadness or even guilt holding you back, just *trying* to protect you.

Self-created illusions

It works the same way with limiting decisions – they may be trying to protect you, but you're not getting the results you deserve. There is only one real emotion on this planet and that is pure love. Now I know it sounds a bit 'new age' but really, to be honest, it *is* just pure love. We strive for love in our lives and what we do in every way, and I'm sure that you know that love is something very powerful to you. Even if we've never had it before, we all want to go ahead and have it, whether it is to love ourselves in every way and have confidence, competence and self-worth. Even love for someone else.

If you have ever been loved, then you know how good it feels. Because all negative emotions are simply manmade – formed by past events or situations that have had an effect on us – and they're simply derivatives of fear in some way. This is good news because it means they're just an illusion.

Negative emotions or beliefs are simply illusions that you're holding right now in your perception. You need to release those, while preserving the powerful teachings from the past, so you can have the knowledge in the now and in the future. And it's a very quick, simple, long-lasting process that will leave you feeling clean and clear of your past negative emotions, limiting decisions and beliefs.

The very first seven years of our lives can be seen as our imprint stage, when everything is being imprinted on us in some way. So all the events that happen around us in the first seven years of life form our personalities, our beliefs and the way that we perceive the world around us. If you think about it, when we are born we are completely pure. We don't have limiting beliefs or negative emotions; we haven't yet contextualized the world around us.

But then, soon enough, as we go through wonderful experiences or even negative experiences, they allow us to form an identity about ourselves and they also form how we perceive the world around us. And that is how we formulate our memories, our personalities, the decisions that we make, the beliefs and values that we hold. So the very first seven years can have a massive impact on our lives.

The next seven years are our modelling stage, and here's where we're actually modelling (or copying) the people around us. We've got the basis of life, we've got the basis of our personalities and our identities, and the way we perceive the world, but then we begin to see people around us and we take on their values, beliefs and attitudes. We look to our peers, our family, our siblings, our friends, our teachers and learn our values and beliefs from them. We might even draw our beliefs and values from people on the radio, on TV, in the movies or in the celebrity world. It can be anyone who we admire and draw on for motivation.

The next seven years is our socialization stage, where we're beginning to socialize and even make our own decisions about life. We're weighing up past events and really formulating what we think we should do. And from 21 onwards, we are adults (although, admittedly, not everyone acts like one).

So, having gone through a series of events in our lives, we will probably have formulated limiting or positive beliefs about the way we perceive our reality. We need to let go of the unhealthy negative things and poor associations we have learned. Because every time you go through a negative event, your unconscious mind labels and remembers it. So every time it goes into a new event it can categorize what is anger, what is sadness, what is fear, what is guilt and so on. So the unconscious mind has a labelling system, like a chain of events that knows this emotion is anger or a chain of events that it recognizes as being sad or happy.

Now what we want to do is clean out all the past negative emotions connected to those events so, when you look back, you can just feel appreciation for all the relevant teachings without having to relive them emotionally. You're literally putting a positive spin on what you've gone through, while gaining the wonderful learning experience. In the future, you'll know that the teachings from your past will support and help you in the most positive and wonderful way.

So, go ahead now and be free of those old unwarranted emotions and beliefs on your list. Go to www.josephclough.com/byp and play or download the *Negative Emotion Release Process*. This hypnosis track will really help you to overcome any negative emotions that you are holding and allow you to approach your life with a fresh perspective.

Recap

- Say 'I love you', as often as you can, but also 'Forgive me', 'I'm sorry' and 'Thank you' – four phrases guaranteed to transform your world. Applying these simple yet powerful words will dissolve conflict and allow you to realize the beauty of yourself, other people and life itself.

- The mind and body hold onto negative emotions such as anger, sadness, fear, guilt and hurt as a form of protection. However, when we learn from our past, those teachings protect us and allow the negative emotion to disappear.

- When we clear out past emotions and limiting decisions, while preserving the lessons they have taught us, we can be truly aligned with where we wish to be in the now and in the future.

Be Your Potential.

CHAPTER FIVE

YOUR JOURNEY HAS JUST BEGUN

In the last chapter we talked about 'getting clear' and I trust you listened to the Negative Emotion Release Process *and 'cleared out' all your limiting beliefs and past negative feelings. This is such a valuable and important process if you want to become aligned with your desired outcomes. Let go of those negative attachments and associations, limiting decisions or beliefs, so you can be clean and clear – so that nothing can stop you from achieving your goals.*

The five principles of success

So, now you have the ability to get rid of negative emotions and limiting decisions, it's very important that you also know the steps to success. And to me, the principles of success are very easy to understand. And there's only five principles or steps.

1. Know your outcome.

2. Take inspired action.

3. Have awareness.

4. Be flexible in your behaviour.

5. Operate from a physiological and psychological state of excellence.

Let's go through each one in detail.

1. Know your outcome

By now, I hope you realize how important it is to know your outcome – to know what you want – and more importantly, to know it in the positive tense. Because if you don't, you're getting your mind and body to continuously focus on what you don't want. All the clients I see – whatever their particular issue or current status – tend to say to me, 'I just don't want this to happen – I don't want to feel bad about myself,' or 'I don't want to have a panic attack in this situation'. Now if you're sending the signals of 'panic attack', sending the signals of 'bad relationships' or 'poor health', even if you don't want them consciously, if you're thinking of them and creating images of them in your mind and feeling fearful or negative toward that outcome of what you don't want, your mind is still focusing on it.

So you've got to change your level of focus onto what you *do* want. It's okay if you have those negative thoughts or perceptions from time to time, but you've got to be conscious of them, and when you become conscious that you're focusing on what you don't want, then you've got to change your focus.

The only reason you have doubting thoughts and fears is to tell you that you haven't reached your goal *yet* – which is a great intention and signal to refocus consciously back on your desired outcomes. As long as you're conscious of the negative thoughts, you can change them and flip them straight back to the positive outcome. Because if your mind is in sync with your outcome – and you're visualizing the goal in your mind every day with consistency and you're having powerful, strong emotions towards your outcome – your mind and body become in sync and aligned in getting it. So it's valuable to really make sure that you *know your outcome* and make sure it's exactly how you want it!

Now I really believe that everyone knows what outcome they want. Even though a lot of people say they don't know what will happen or what their outcome will be, actually they only know what they don't want. I still believe that everyone has that purpose or outcome in mind at an unconscious and maybe even a conscious level.

Unfortunately, there will still be some parts of you wanting to stay where you are. Now I don't mean necessarily consciously, although sometimes that can be true, but it may just be at an unconscious level.

Many people sometimes feel conflicted. On the one hand they say, 'I really want to be able to (fill in the blank)'. But no matter how much they want it on the one hand, there's that slight bit of doubt, negative feeling, association or even past memory telling them that they can't – they become conflicted towards achieving their goals or outcomes. For example, they might say:

'I really want a promotion – but I fear failure.'

'I want to be free of dis-ease – but I'm not worthy of having good health.'

'I'd love to be rich – but I don't think I am intelligent enough.'

'I want to have a loving relationship – but I'm not attractive enough.'

Now if this is the case with you, I want you to do this for a second. I want you to think of that part of you, which is stopping you from getting your result, and then I want you to imagine it in your mind, envisage how it would be. As if it has a symbolic representation in some way – how would you imagine it? How would it be? Would it be a voice, a feeling, an image or someone you know?

Then I want you to imagine asking that part of you: *For what purpose are you running that behaviour/ feeling/conflict?* Remember, there is always a positive intention for your internal conflict, belief, doubt or negative emotion.

For example, the intention of a phobia is to protect – although the behaviour itself rarely protects the person's mental wellbeing. Phobias are like a small child drawing on your brand new wallpaper. His or her intention is to draw you a nice picture, so the purpose/intention is good but the behaviour is unhelpful.

I want you to honour your good intention but to release the negative thought, belief, feeling or behaviour and get back in alignment with your outcome. You may get nothing at first, and that's fine because you haven't asked that type of question before. So keep asking 'for what purpose' and notice what comes up. Ask yourself:

'For what purpose are you running that belief or behaviour or feeling?'

Your intention is going to be positive in some way, as your unconscious is trying to help or protect you – even though your behaviour in response may be unhelpful. For example, the word 'protection' may come up, or 'fear of failure', or 'not good enough', or 'not wanting to look silly' or 'not wanting to risk losing everything'.

Whatever your answer, just trust your unconscious and take whatever answer comes up.

Notice the answer and when you notice the purpose or the intention behind that conflict, I want you to say 'thank you' and then ask your unconscious again: 'For what purpose do you want that for me?' In other words, 'For what purpose – protection?' Notice what comes up, and then say, 'Thank you for that intention – for what purpose do you want that?' Keep asking these questions – going up higher and higher – until you reach its highest intention.

Now your unconscious mind's highest intention will always, and I mean always, be absolutely good for you. If you keep asking those questions – 'for what purpose' or 'for what intention' – even if you get no answers for a while, you will notice that eventually you'll get into a higher state of wellbeing. You may come up with words such as 'wholeness', 'contentment', 'happiness', 'a better life', 'to be the real me'. Whatever it is, keep going until you reach those states and answers in your mind. Because that part is only running that behaviour, thought, belief, memory or feeling for a positive intention.

Your unconscious mind is performing to its best ability at present: it thinks this behaviour is the correct way to act or react due to your past experiences and decisions. It's running the issue with the best of intentions for you. For example, if your problem is 'fear of failure', then your dialogue may run as follows:

Question: *For what purpose 'fear of failure'?*

Answer: *Protection.*

Question: *For what purpose 'protection'?*

Answer: *To remain safe.*

Question: *For what purpose 'remain safe'?*

Answer: *To perform.*

Question: *For what purpose 'to perform'?*

Answer: *To be okay in all situations.*

Question: *For what purpose 'to be okay in all situations'?*

Answer: *To be happy.*

Question: *For what purpose 'to be happy'?*

Answer: *To be the real me.*

So the original problem was 'fear of failure', but the unconscious mind's highest intention for running the belief was 'to be the real me'.

By doing this process you are breaking out of your unconscious mind's present belief, feeling or behaviour. When this happens your unconscious mind realizes the problem is not achieving its highest intention in 'being the real me'. Your unconscious mind then has to re-evaluate the problem and come up with a new belief, feeling or behaviour that achieves its own highest intention – 'being the real me'. For example: 'I can achieve anything if I put my mind to it'.

The reason there is a conflict is that part of you is 'stuck'. It has just not grown up or learned from the weeks, months and years gone by since the problem was created. I want that part of you to now understand that the outcome you desire is going to get everything the 'negative' part wants – e.g. the safety – but also the happiness and contentment of achieving your dreams and being the real you.

So if some issues ever come up in the future from within, you can use the process 'I love you', 'Thank you', 'Forgive me' and 'I'm sorry', while also using the questioning process by asking: 'For what purpose are you running this behaviour? For what purpose do you have this feeling for me?' In doing these processes, you're re-establishing communication with your unconscious mind – the part running the behaviour. You are making the unconscious conscious of your true desires and letting go of all conflicts that are in the way of them.

This process of saying 'for what purpose' or 'for what intention' is actually going to get you more wholeness and contentment in life. This part or 'block' in your unconscious has been holding you back. But there was a time when you didn't have it – maybe when you were newborn, maybe at five or ten years old. It doesn't really matter when it happened, but for some reason it happened – it was formulated in some way.

We've got to break through the neurological boundary of that belief, feeling or emotion. So by asking your unconscious mind 'for what purpose' and 'for what intention' until it gets to its highest intention (which is always absolutely positive), it will break out of that neurological boundary and it won't be able to function in the same manner again. It will be developing more wholeness by integrating into the 'whole you' in every way.

So this process really helps in producing and knowing your outcome and getting aligned to your outcome. And once again, you may be thinking, 'I don't know my purpose or what outcomes that I want in the positive'. But let's break this down a little bit.

Maybe you want to have love, a fulfilling life, experience happiness, to be wealthy, have fame, to feel good enough, to feel accepted or achieve the perfect health. Even if it's as ambiguous as that, it'll give you a starting point of knowing what you want. Unfortunately, before now, you have been acting and reacting from programmed memories rather than 'inspired action'. That is what stops us from knowing our outcome.

So now it's time to reconnect and remember what you want. And if you recall from Chapter 3, we played with the idea of having Godlike powers, so if you could do anything, be anything or have anything, what would it be? And then that will begin to actualize your outcome. By having the mindset of having Godlike powers, you are freeing yourself of limitations, you are freeing yourself from the constraints of those past programmed memories – you're thinking outside the box.

So think about it, what do you want? And state it in the positive.

What you're doing right now is what Carl Jung described as 'making the unconscious conscious'. The majority of what's happening inside you right now is being run at an unconscious level. We probably only have about 10 per cent conscious control of being aligned with our goals and outcomes. All the rest is being run at an unconscious level – our beliefs, values, our personality types, our decisions and our memories of the past. Now we're just really getting you to be conscious of your unconscious, and allowing your unconscious to be conscious.

Know your outcome.

2. Take inspired action

The second principle is to take action. Don't do it in the same way as you've always done, but take 'inspired action'. It's not positive to do something that makes you feel as if it's not being you or to feel uncomfortable about taking the decision – it's got to be inspired.

You can't just sit there and do nothing: it doesn't work that way. You've got to take action that makes you feel good. Even if you don't know what the steps are yet, it's about taking those initial steps of thinking and knowing your outcome. Then your unconscious mind will allow you to see the opportunities and you will know what steps you need to take next. You'll begin to perceive new opportunities and adventures to know what to do and get your outcome. So taking action is essential.

Anyone who has achieved anything in life has had to take action in some way. So now knowing your outcome, you have to now take action – let it be inspired action.

We must take action, seize the moment and do what we desire. Without action, we are simply dreamers, but by taking active steps we are visionaries manifesting dreams into reality. It's time for you to assume the feeling of having achieved your desires, and then take action with conviction. When you decide to do this, you decide to live. It's no good just meditating or visualizing achieving your outcomes, as that alone will not get you anywhere. You must instigate and maintain change and develop actions that, once carried out, move you towards your outcome.

Think: *What three actions can I do every day, every week that will move me towards my outcome?* Then commit to doing them. It all starts with your thoughts, but you must take them into actual behaviours that consistently produce results towards achieving your outcome. This will move you beyond your comfort zone at times, but remember, everything you have ever done was once out of your comfort zone.

It's all about moving forwards. Never stand still, because if you are not growing you are dying. Push yourself to learn more, to better yourself and to grow. This is your life, your reality and you deserve the best, but only you can give yourself permission to step forwards and live it. As Martin Luther King so eloquently said, 'You may not see the whole staircase, you just have to take the first step.'

Let your action be inspired by your outcome.

3. Have awareness

Having awareness is about being and knowing what you're doing, and if it's not working, to do something else. Many of my clients have done the exact same thing they've always done, still trying to get their outcome and hitting a brick wall. To me, that's just silly. You need to vary your actions and know that what you're doing isn't achieving the outcome yet.

So if your action is not working, do something different. No matter what it is, just do something different until you get that success.

You've got to have awareness of what's working and what isn't. Once you know it's not working, simply do something else. By awareness I also mean to become conscious of your thoughts, feelings and behaviours, as they dictate the results you get. Albert Einstein once defined 'insanity' as 'doing the same thing over and over again and expecting different results'.

To be successful we have to be aware of the results we are getting. I don't want you to *take inspired action* and just get the same results of not getting your goal. You have to be aware and conscious of the results you are getting. You can become conscious by asking yourself the questions: *Is what I am doing getting me closer to my goal? What other actions can I take that will yield the results I desire?*

Cultivate your thoughts, feelings and behaviours, because the more you become conscious and aware of your actions, the more you can refine them. We can become so engrossed or entranced by the daily business of just living that we forget to stop and consider where we are, where we are heading, and furthermore, the steps we are making. The chances are you that picked up this book because you want to better yourself in some way, to grow as a person and be happy. That is having awareness, but you must have awareness about your behaviours too. It's important to really wake up to this step, as it allows you to grow as a person and achieve your goals.

Be aware of what isn't working and do something else.

4. Be flexible in your behaviour

Behavioural flexibility simply means that if you know your behaviour isn't working, then be flexible and behave differently.

So you know your outcome, you are taking action and are aware of the results you are getting. If they are not the results you want then change your behaviour, be flexible in your environment.

Think of it this way: you are alive today because your ancestors were able to adjust their behaviour – to overcome environmental changes, illnesses and viruses – in order not just to survive but also to thrive. Other species have not been so lucky as they failed to adapt to their environment. But your biological body did, and now you must take that level of flexibility into your psychological mindset.

Changing your behaviours to thrive in the environment means having behavioural flexibility, adjusting your behaviour to overcome challenges, to overcome the odds and to succeed. The person with the most flexibility controls the situation, as they're able to adjust their mindset and their feelings to make sure they can still perform well and do something different to achieve their success. So, for example, don't be attached to one specific way of getting or achieving something. What other ways could it be done? Think outside the box and trust your gut instinct on the right way to achieve your goal.

When we are rigid and closed to change we stop growing. However, when we develop flexibility in our behaviour, it means we can adjust and learn from our experience – we can learn from what life throws at us.

One way of doing this is to reflect on any past actions that didn't work out the way you intended – don't dwell on them but do learn from them. Ask yourself: *What can I learn from this, which once learned, will allow me to adapt and get better? How can I improve? What other actions can I take?* Those teachings will be with you as you adapt your behaviour to achieve your goal.

Be flexible and trust your instinct.

5. Operate from a physiological and psychological state of excellence

Acquiring a state of physiological and psychological excellence is the purpose of this book. If you're thinking positively and feeling good, and your thoughts and feelings are in alignment towards your outcome – with all the feelings of gratitude, trust, love, confidence and wellbeing – your physiology will begin to change. We know that if you have a healthy mind you get a healthy body, and we also know if you have a healthy body you're going to get a healthy mind. So it's important to act as if you have these right now. Trust me, if you *act* the way that you want to be, your unconscious mind will begin to do it naturally for you – it becomes a habit at a neurological level.

So if you think and act with a physiological and psychological state of excellence, you're going to be more aligned in getting your outcome.

You have to act as if you have it already. Think and feel the way that you want to be in every way. This is called modelling and it really works. So if you know someone who has achieved what you want – whether it is a similar goal, perfect health, the relationships, the finances, or exactly how you want to be – ask them how they did it. Ask them how they perceive their reality, what are they thinking from day to day, what is their mindset and behaviour towards that goal or outcome.

Don't be worried about asking someone for help, because the more you ask for help, advice and support the more likely you will get it in return. Ask anyone who can help you. Many people believe that asking is a negative thing: it may make you feel needy or hurt your pride or make you believe the other person won't have the time. The simple truth is that most people actually want to be needed and liked, and most people enjoy helping others. Be thankful verbally if they've helped you – that's your payment to them and it means more than money. By asking them what they did and asking for help, you are ultimately complimenting them and, if they are like everyone else, they will love talking about themselves. So ask away and figure out their strategy, their mindset and what they did.

Once you've found the required behaviour, you can install it in yourself and act that way. But either way, you've got to act and react from a state of physiological and psychological excellence.

Think and feel your desired outcome with excellence.

Use the audio download (www.josephclough.com/byp) called *Becoming the You, You Wish To Be* to help you get the mindset, resources and behaviours – consciously and unconsciously – to achieve your desired outcome.

Keys to an achievable outcome

Now you know your outcome, and the steps to achieve it, here are the keys to an achievable outcome. You can write your answers in a journal or on your computer (or download the questionnaires from www.josephclough.com/byp), but what's important is that you record your answers so that you can refer to them in the future.

First of all, think and state exactly what you want in the positive.

What specifically do you want? Write this down.

Then you need to specify the present situation.

Where are you now in terms of achieving your goal? Write this down.

This sets the distance between your goal and your present situation. You then know where you are and you know where you're going.

Then you've got to be more specific in achieving your outcome. So write down what you will see, hear and feel when you have your outcome. Whether it relates to your health, relationships, career or finances. Think about it right now.

What would you be seeing? How will you know when

you've got this outcome? What would you be hearing? What would you be feeling? Write this down.

Then, when you think of that picture, which creates a joyful feeling, make it bigger, brighter and more intense. Make the feelings expand inside your awareness, allow that picture to grow really big and be really associated (looking through your own eyes) inside that picture, and allow your internal self-talk to build you up to that feeling of having achieved your outcome.

This is really about thinking about how you will know when you have achieved your outcome. Many people go through life with desired outcomes that they actually achieve, yet they don't recognise it at the time, only in hindsight. I want you to know when it happens, so you can experience the deep inner satisfaction of complete success.

How will you know when you have this outcome? Write this down.

This will tell you that you've achieved your outcome. When I first became a therapist I developed a procedure of always understanding 'what evidence' my clients needed in order to know that they had achieved their goal. It sounds obvious but it's very important to know once you've achieved your desired outcome.

Is the desire congruent? Write this down.

What will this outcome get for you and allow you to do? Write this down

So for what purpose do you want this outcome? Write this down.

Is it good for you, is it good for your environment and is it good for others? Write this down.

The more that it is good for you and the people around you, the more beneficial that outcome will be and therefore be manifested into your life.

Is it self-initiated and self-maintained by you? Write this down.

We've got to make sure that you initiate it, that you're the goal-getter.

Where do you want this outcome in your life? Write this down.

When do you want it? Write this down.

How would you like it to happen? Write this down.

And with whom do you want it? Write this down.

When do you want to achieve your outcome – maybe tomorrow, maybe next week? Obviously it's got to be a smart goal – specific, measurable, achievable, realistic (which depends on your definition of realistic) and time involved. So where do you want it? When do you want it?

And do you need any resources? Write this down.

What do you have now and what do you need to get this outcome? Write this down.

Have you ever had or done this before? Write this down.

Do you know anyone who has, so you can begin to model them? Write this down.

Can you act as if you have it right now? Write this down.

Once again, we've got to make sure we're in balance. And the following questions will be able to change how you perceive the outcome – even if it feels confusing at first.

So for what purpose do you want this? Write this down.

What will you gain or lose if you get this outcome? Write this down.

What will happen if you get it? Write this down.

What won't happen if you get it? Write this down.

And then the final two, which will really begin to shift your viewpoint.

What will happen if you don't get it? Write this down.

We're really setting up the boundaries here, the real context of the situation.

What won't happen if you don't get it? Write this down.

So these are the keys to achieving your outcomes. You can go over this list of questions any time you wish to really make sure that you're aligned with your outcomes. Usually people just have thoughts or feelings about their outcomes but they don't know the real context of the situation, they don't know how they want it to happen or when they want it to happen. By writing this down, or just thinking in this way, you'll begin to get a clear image in your mind of how you're going to achieve your outcomes.

Creating a timeline of your life

Now the next two processes are truly wonderful. It really amazes me how accurate this process is in manifesting our goals and outcomes. Let me tell you a story.

When I first started out I wanted to truly transform people's lives, so I set myself some goals – the type of things I wanted to achieve – and broke them down into certain categories.

- Business: career goals I want to achieve.

- Family: how I'd like my relationships to be with my family.

- Friends: how I wanted my friendships to be.

- Myself: my own personal goals and behaviour.

- Assets: the type of assets I'd like to have at certain periods of my life.

And I began to write a list of the types of things that I wanted, how I wanted them and how I wanted my life to be. But there was a problem. I kept on thinking it would happen in the next 12 months, or it would happen in the next two or three years. In other words, it was always future-based. But I quickly realized this meant I'd always be living for the future. And, as I pointed out earlier in the book, living for the future creates its own problems and won't bring you immediate happiness.

We've got to make sure we know the future, but we've got to start living in the *now* to truly achieve all our outcomes and goals – and enjoy every present moment. And once I got around this problem of always perceiving it would happen in the future, everything seemed to change. My outcomes began ppen much quicker, because I'd be thinking and ing it happening now.

And when I had that feeling of gratitude for all the things that I wanted, and I knew they were going to happen to me in the coming days, weeks and months – at the most within the next six months – they started to happen in that time period. So on the one hand it is good to have a plan of your future, but I don't want you to get in the mindset of thinking about the future all the time. It's about living now as well as knowing what's going to happen in the future.

So here's the process. I've filled out an example below for you and then it will be your turn to jot down your age and what age you'll be in 25 years' time. I'd suggest using categories for business, family, friends, self and assets and you can always add more categories, but the most important thing is to write down as much detail as possible. (You can download a PDF of this process from www.josephclough.com/byp.) So let's go through some of the outcomes I wrote down when I first started my journey in 2004. In 25 years' time (where I am, what I'm doing and what I've got) being 46.

Business

- Internationally known trainer.

- I do many seminars, trainings and talks.

- I have written five books.

- I am hired by top corporate businesses to assist them in improving and maintaining success within their business, from sales to goal setting.

- I still see clients – celebrities and the general public – with mental health issues and help people every day. I usually command a fee of up to £10,000 per day, as I get the results needed. I do voluntary work and donate large amounts of money to charity.

- I earn £2,000,000 per year after tax in relation to 2004 currency.

- I am involved in TV and radio work.

Family

- Happily married for 16 years and extremely in love with my wife, who's my soul mate, best friend and guide – as I am hers – and our love grows more each day.

- We have three children who are bright, loving and passionate about life.

- I have a close loving family. I keep in touch and see my mum, dad and brothers as often as I can, and we have a warm, understanding relationship.

- I get on with my brothers like good friends and even have business arrangements with them.

Friends

- I have close friends working in the same field that I enjoy spending time with. We write and train together, and discuss ways of transforming lives.

- I still see my oldest friends occasionally and we have great connections.

Self

- I am growing with each day – learning more and more about the world and expanding my mind.

- I am a spiritual and wise person, and I feel very whole.

- I am very business-minded.

- I am very down to earth and I can relate and communicate on all levels.

- I am physically and mentally very well and healthy.

- I look much younger than my age.

- I practice what I teach and look and produce great ways in developing myself.

- I am a leader, teacher, student and guide.

Assets

- I have £3,000,000 in savings.

- I have four homes, one in or around London with five bedrooms, a swimming pool and a big garden, and an estate in the country.

- I have two up-to-date sports cars (Porsche) and one family car.

- I have profitable investments in properties and businesses.

Now in a moment, I'd like you to start your list detailing where you'll be in 25 years' time. Write down your age in 25 years' time and then a list of points under each heading – aim for a minimum of five points under each heading. Then do the same exercise for 15 years' time, then seven years' time, three years' time, one year's time and six months, working all the way back.

Now the reason you're writing these goals backwards is that once you know your end outcome – your design for how you want your life to be – you can then backtrack the steps to make sure you can achieve all those goals. If you start from six or 12 months' time it would be difficult to know how to get those goals, but if you start at the end goal, you can then backtrack to make sure you know what to do and how to get it. Everyone I know who has used this exercise has noticed some amazing things. The idea is to write down your goals and then occasionally check in with your list to make sure that your present action is aligned with your future goals. Most people find that when they do check their list, they have achieved the majority of the goals they wrote down

– and in most cases they weren't even consciously thinking about them. It's as if once you have written your list, your unconscious mind and conscious mind naturally search for those outcomes and goals.

For example, my father Paul did this process many years ago and wrote down that he wanted a boat by a specific age, and when he looked back many years later, he realized that he achieved a boat in the year that he wrote down. But guess what, he forgot about his list – he forgot about actually writing down that he wanted a boat. But it still, at an unconscious level, manifested into his life.

And I know for a fact that when I've done this process, I'm on track with my goals in my life. It's as if you're writing your own script for the rest of your life. It allows your mind to begin to focus on the things that you want, and once again, if you're focusing on what you want, your unconscious mind will begin to search for the answers to make it happen. So this is a wonderful process to actually carry out.

What I'd like you to do is to write down all your 'outcomes' in your chosen categories, so by the end of the week you have produced all the things that you would like to achieve. And make sure these goals you're setting are big goals, in the sense that if you achieve those goals it will truly change your life. Remember to think 'Godlike'.

I can't build this process up enough – not only is it fun, it's like creating your own shopping list of how you want your life to be, but strangely enough the results really happen at an unconscious level. Doing this process also means that you're starting to take responsibility for your goals by owning your life, owning each area of your life and making sure it actualizes into your life.

Remember, be bold with what you want!

Your ultimate vision

The next thing I want you to do is make a vision board, which simply means taking a sheet of paper and putting images of the things that you want in your life – your goals – on it. So if you really want a nice car, go ahead and find a picture of it and stick it on your piece of paper – your vision board. And then you might include the house that you'd like and the things that you'd like to achieve. Include the salary you want by taking a bank statement and changing the date and the amount with a pen so that it's postdated and with the desired amount in your bank balance by then.

You might include pictures of holidays, wonderful houses, maybe your ideal soul mate or maybe your perfect health. Find an image for anything that you want, cut it out and stick it on your vision board.

I've done this process, and once again the results are magnificent. By creating this vision board – by putting pictures of all the things I really want to achieve – I've noticed that those things actually manifest in my life and I've achieved many of them. And I've even taken this further, so every time I turn on my computer I see all the pictures, all the things that I actually want to achieve, on my desktop background. I now can't escape my dreams – they're right in front of me.

So why is it important to create a vision board of all the wonderful goals you want to achieve? Well here's the key – every time you look at your vision board it reminds you consciously and unconsciously to go ahead and achieve those outcomes. It keeps your desired outcomes fresh in your mind and you create positive visualizations of achieving those outcomes. So every time you see that piece of paper, you're stepping up your vibrations to be in alignment of those goals. Rather than out of sight, out of mind, you're putting your goals at the forefront of your mind so you can actively seek out how to get them.

This is a creative process, because it's all about you and exactly what you want.

I really believe that you deserve to achieve your outcomes. Okay, you haven't got them at the moment, but it's now time to change that around and take responsibility back in your life. You deserve to have the most wonderful health, the most loving relationships and financial abundance. You deserve all those things and even more. And by allowing this process to be in the forefront of your mind, you're literally creating your future. You're keeping your mind congruent and aligned with what you want. Sometimes we focus on the things that we don't want – which, as we've discovered, doesn't work.

These processes allow your focus to be exactly where you want it. Having that precise focus, exactly how you want it, will raise your vibrations. It will allow your feelings to guide your thoughts and your thoughts to guide your ways of acting and reacting. To truly change your present reality into the reality you desire – the real you and exactly how you want it.

Recap

- Know your outcome – focus on the positive outcome you desire. The conscious mind is the goal-setter and the unconscious mind is the goal-getter. Allow your thoughts and feelings to reflect your desires, knowing they will become the guide to your unconscious mind.

- Take action – take inspired and massive action. When you start to do, you start to get. What steps can you take today that will move you closer to your goal? Act upon those steps with conviction.

- Have awareness – become conscious of the

results you are getting. If it's not working then ask yourself: *What else can I do? What have I not done, that if I did would allow me to move forward?* It's time to wake up to your internal and external behaviours and cultivate them to create success.

- Show behavioural flexibility – be flexible, adjust, modify and evolve as a human being each step of the way. If you don't succeed by taking a certain action, remember there is no failure, just feedback that once learned we can use the teaching in the future. Ask yourself the following: *What can I learn from this that will allow me to adapt and get better? How can I improve? What other actions can I take?* Be flexible and trust your instincts.

- Operate from a state of physiological and psychological excellence – assume the thoughts and feelings of having achieved your goal and act upon them with conviction.

- Your past actions have led you to this point, but your present actions lead you to where you are going in the future. It all starts in this moment.

Be Your Potential.

THE ENDING AND
THE BEGINNING AGAIN

People will only ever change when they are aware of a problem in their lives. Most people around the world are asleep to their present unhappiness: they think it is a normal state to be in. They believe that the chain of anxiety, fears, worries and low self-esteem is not only a way of life but a part of their identity.

This book was written to tell you that this isn't and shouldn't be the case. Forces in society spread fear, and worries about not being good enough. I am here to whisper a thought in your ear. To wake you up from the illusion of the pursuit of happiness: there is no pursuit needed. Happiness does not come from doing, but from being. You have everything you need to make the changes you want, and the journey should not be one of just external processes but rather an internal process.

The fact that you are perhaps aware of an issue in your life means you are waking up to the solution. Rather than being caged by thinking that it's just the way of life, instead you are being conscious that there must be a way to achieve your goals and another way of being happy. When you get to that place you are taking responsibility and switching your attention to what you want, and that causes your mind to look for the answers within.

We can only be kept in the cages we cannot see

Now you are seeing the illusionary cage (the problem), all you have to do is put your attention firmly on what you want and become it.

At the end of the day, *things* happen. Life throws obstacles at us thick and fast, but it's not what comes to us that is the issue, it's how we respond to it. When life throws us trauma it can allow us to know who we are. It causes us to dig deep within us, to look within to the deepest part of who we are. It enables us to go to places that we have never been. Here is the counterintuitive part: I remember when I was sad, unconfident and not good enough and although it took me a long time to know the truth, I am so happy and grateful to have had my issues. I am grateful to have blushed chronically, to have felt unworthy and not good enough.

If I hadn't gone through those experiences, I wouldn't be who I am or have achieved my aspirations or know what it is like to truly live. But more importantly, beyond all of that and the path I have taken, it has allowed me to realize who I am.

Everything is a choice – we choose everything and you are not here to be a bit-part player.

Who are you? What are you not? My truth

Let me start by saying what you are not. You are not anxiety, you are not depression, you are not low confidence and you are not fear. These are all behaviours you have picked up, only behaviours, and you are not your behaviours. You are not small, weak or limited. You are not the lack of life, you are not just part of life. You are not your thoughts and you are definitely not powerless. You are not your excuses, you are not your reasons, you are not everything that is wrong and you are not the problem. You are not a product of your environment. You are not any of those things.

So what are you?

You are everything you need, you are choice, you are abundant and you are potential. When we go back to what we truly are, we are peace, made of love and whole.

The trouble is that we have learned to direct our awareness to those things that we think are real – the things we need to buy, or buying into what we should be because society says so. But you are not 'meant' to be anything. You are just you: you are beauty, peace, love, happiness, contentment, joy and bliss. The whole idea that you are meant to be a certain way presupposes that you are not okay and you need to move to somewhere else to be okay. But you are not meant to be anything other than what is you – pure amazing potential.

Rather than being a product of your environment, your environment is one you choose to create.

The deeper part of you knows this, it always has. I think we all know this, but many of us get lost along the way. So how do we get found? We must awaken to what is already here. There is nowhere to go but here, now, in this moment. You must be conscious and aware of what you are: you are love and peace; you are perfect – not the perfect we may have learned to expect, but nevertheless perfect and beautiful. In order to do this, we need to remember this:

- Give up our limitations and make the choice to no longer 'buy' into reasons why we are like we are. When we do this, we change our focus from scarcity and lack to infinite possibilities of potential.

- Our present situation is governed by our past actions and decisions, but our future is governed by what we do now in the present – it all starts right now!

- When negative thoughts come to mind, it's our signal to focus on what we have (be grateful/ attitude of gratitude and consider all the opposites of the negative). To break free of past- and future-based thinking by living in the now.

- The mind is a reflection of the outer world. We can allow ourselves to be a product of what life is, or allow life to be a product of what we are – you choose.

- The process of getting what we want is about knowing our outcome and taking the three steps – ask, believe and receive.

Once more, the keys to success are to:

1. Know your outcome.

2. Take inspired action.

3. Have awareness.

4. Be flexible in your behaviour.

5. Operate from a physiological and psychological state of excellence.

When you put your attention to the inner world of you, you change the outer reality of you and the results you get, as well as those around you. This is an opportunity to give up your excuses and limitations. This is your time to say, 'This is my life, I am the creator, the instigator, the person who makes things happen.' You are not limited – which may be our greatest fear – it is just an illusion; the truth is that you are unlimited. You are powerful.

It's no longer impossible – it's probable.

A beautiful journey

So this is the end of this book, but your journey has just begun and I want you to carry on allowing your focus to guide you to where you want to be. Allow yourself to take responsibility for the situation. Rather than being a product of what life gives you, allow life to be a product of what you are.

Everything you see in the world around you, allow it to be a product of something that you've manifested. From now on, you own your situation and your life. Allow yourself to focus on your outcomes and allow your feelings and actions to guide you there. And if you have negative thoughts or feelings, be conscious of them and make them simply disappear. Then continue to focus on exactly what you want to achieve.

And focus on exactly the positive outcomes that you want. Allow yourself to have that feeling of gratitude every time you wake up in the morning. Write down those ten wonderful things that you feel truly thankful for – that you feel truly prosperous for.

Allow those feelings to carry on throughout the whole day, enabling your mind to be in sync with the type of life that you deserve – a life which has all the love and the most wonderful, beautiful relationships, the most profound good health and wellbeing. Even having financial security in abundance to help yourself and others around you. Remember, everything that you do, make sure it's good for yourself and others.

The results you're going to produce will be truly transformational, but I want you to be able to touch other people's lives too. I want you to allow yourself to give more out into this world and therefore gain much more because of it.

Have trust and just know that you're going to get your outcome. Reawaken your belief and wonder inside and allow those feelings to manifest so you can graciously receive all the abundance you deserve.

Continue to hold the pictures and feelings in your mind of your goals. Every night when you go to sleep, think and feel all the things you want to achieve. Keep those thoughts and images throughout the whole day because this will allow your energy, your vibrations, your thoughts and your feelings to truly manifest as you become your own potential.

Allow your life to be a beautiful journey that you love. Allow everything you do to become something you have created – this is *your* journey. I'm glad you've accepted and allowed me to be a part of your journey. And I can't wait to hear exactly how you've got on in manifesting the reality that you deserve to have. Because you truly deserve it, I know that for a fact.

Now it's time to start living your life the way that you've always wanted it – the way that you wanted it as a child – free of limitations. It's no longer impossible, it's probable now, and if you choose, it can be definite. It's only a matter of time before you will be living to your true potential.

But one thing is important in allowing this to happen – *that is you!*

You can take all the credit for allowing this process to happen right now.

By taking responsibility for your life, you can take all the credit for having achieved your goals and outcomes very soon.

You are here to shine, here to grow and to be your potential.

**With love,
Joseph**

HAY HOUSE TITLES OF RELATED INTEREST

9 Days to Feel Fantastic: How to Create
Happiness from the Inside Out,
by John Whiteman

The 10 Questions to Ask for Success,
by Phil Parker

Change Your Words, Change Your World,
by Andrea Gardner

The Contagious Power of Thinking: How
Your Thoughts Can Influence the World,
by David R. Hamilton PhD

The Fire Starter Sessions,
by Danielle LaPorte

How Long is Now?: How to be Spiritually
Awake in the Real World,
by Tim Freke

Shift Happens: How to Live an Inspired Life
Starting from Now!,
by Robert Holden PhD

Supercoach: 10 Secrets To Transform Anyone's Life,
by Michael Neill

We hope you enjoyed this Hay House book. If you'd like to receive our online catalogue featuring additional information on Hay House books and products, or if you'd like to find out more about the Hay Foundation, please contact:

Hay House UK, Ltd., Astley House, 33 Notting Hill Gate
Phone: 0-20-3675-2450 • Fax: 0-20-3675-2451
www.hayhouse.co.uk • **www.hayfoundation.org**

Published and distributed in the United States by:
Hay House, Inc., P.O. Box 5100, Carlsbad, CA 92018-5100
Phone: (760) 431-7695 or (800) 654-5126
Fax: (760) 431-6948 or (800) 650-5115
www.hayhouse.com®

Published and distributed in Australia by:
Hay House Australia Pty. Ltd., 18/36 Ralph St., Alexandria NSW 2015
Phone: 612-9669-4299 • *Fax:* 612-9669-4144 • www.hayhouse.com.au

Published and distributed in the Republic of South Africa by:
Hay House SA (Pty), Ltd., P.O. Box 990, Witkoppen 2068
Phone/Fax: 27-11-467-8904 • www.hayhouse.co.za

Published in India by: Hay House Publishers India,
Muskaan Complex, Plot No. 3, B-2, Vasant Kunj,
New Delhi 110 070 • *Phone:* 91-11-4176-1620
Fax: 91-11-4176-1630 • www.hayhouse.co.in

Distributed in Canada by: Raincoast,
9050 Shaughnessy St., Vancouver, B.C. V6P 6E5
Phone: (604) 323-7100 • *Fax:* (604) 323-2600 • www.raincoast.com

Take Your Soul on a Vacation

Visit www.HealYourLife.com® to regroup,
recharge, and reconnect with your own magnificence.
Featuring blogs, mind-body-spirit news, and
life-changing wisdom from Louise Hay and friends.

Visit www.HealYourLife.com today!

ABOUT THE AUTHOR

Joseph Clough is a transformational speaker, coach and hypnotherapist. His mission is to help as many people in the world as possible so everyone can live a life of happiness and freedom. Joseph has helped more than 700,000 people in recent years by recording over 100 hours of life-changing audio and giving them away for free so everyone can have the opportunity to be their potential.

Joseph was once a shy child: throughout school he struggled with low confidence, blushing and self-consciousness. He left school at 17, and at 18 years old he was lost, confused and stuck in a job he hated, with nowhere to turn. At his lowest point, he made a decision to do whatever it took to change his situation. He went on a mission to discover the power of the mind, immersing himself in every book he could read on self-help, going on self-development courses and researching the inner workings of the mind. Upon his journey of transforming his own life, being free of blushing and unleashing the power of his true self, for a decade he has worked with clients and has run seminars internationally to show others how they can do the same. He has worked with top celebrities and appeared on ITV1's *Fear Factor*, removing phobias in just ten minutes. At only 28 years old, Joseph is a living example of how anyone can change their life and he is dedicating in show you to make your dreams a reality. As he says, 'Rather being a product of life, allow life to be a product of you.'

You can connect with Joseph at www.josephclough.com, and interact with him on Facebook www.facebook.com/josephsfanpage and Twitter www.twitter.com/josephclough to get access to his free eight-hour confidence programme or download his free Hypnosis iPhone and Android App, which has over 30 free downloadable titles.